Customary Measures of Length

To change a large unit, such as feet, to a smaller unit, such as inches, you multiply.

To change a small unit, such as inches, to a larger unit, such as feet, you divide. Reduce fractions to lowest terms.

$3\frac{1}{2}$ ft. = _____ in. 18 in. = _____ ft.

To change to a smaller unit, multiply.	To change to a larger unit, divide. Reduce if possible.
1 ft. = 12 in.	1 ft. = 12 in.
$3\frac{1}{2} \times 12 = \frac{7}{2} \times \frac{\cancel{12}^6}{1} = 42$ in.	$18 \div 12 = 1\frac{6}{12} = 1\frac{1}{2}$ ft.

Change each measurement to the smaller unit.

1. 6 yd. = __18__ ft. $8\frac{1}{3}$ ft. = _____ in.   3 mi. = _____ ft.
   1 yd. = 3 ft.
   6 × 3 = 18 ft.

2. $4\frac{1}{4}$ ft. = _____ in. $\frac{1}{3}$ yd. = _____ ft.   5 mi. = _____ yd.

3. $\frac{1}{2}$ mi. = _____ yd.   2 yd. = _____ in. $1\frac{2}{3}$ yd. = _____ ft.

Change each measurement to the larger unit. Reduce fractions if possible.

4. 40 in. = $3\frac{1}{3}$ ft.   16 ft. = _____ yd.   2,640 yd. = _____ mi.
   1 ft. = 12 in.
   $40 \div 12 = 3\frac{4}{12} = 3\frac{1}{3}$ ft.

5. 4 ft. = _____ yd.   14 in. = _____ ft.   50 in. = _____ yd.

6. 10,560 ft. = _____ mi.   12 in. = _____ yd.   36 ft. = _____ yd.

Solve.

7. A board is 6 feet long. How many inches is 6 feet?

   Answer _____

8. A driveway is 30 feet long. How many yards is 30 feet?

   Answer _____

Customary Measures of Weight

The table lists common customary units of measurement for weight. The table shows how ounces, pounds, and tons are related to each other. These relationships make it possible to change from one unit to another.

Measures of Weight
1 pound (lb.) = 16 ounces (oz.)
1 ton (T.) = 2,000 lb.

1 lb. = _____ oz. _____ lb. = 1 oz.

To find an equivalent whole unit, use the table.

1 lb. = **16** oz. and **16** oz. = 1 lb.

To find an equivalent fractional unit, divide.

1 lb. = **16** oz.

$\frac{1 \text{ lb.}}{16} = \frac{16 \text{ oz.}}{16}$

$\frac{1}{16}$ lb. = 1 oz. and 1 oz. = $\frac{1}{16}$ lb.

Find the following equivalent whole units.

1. __1__ lb. = 16 oz.   16 oz. = _____ lb.   1 T. = _____ lb.

2. 1 lb. = _____ oz.   _____ oz. = 1 lb.   2,000 lb. = _____ T.

Find the following equivalent fractional units.

3. 1 oz. = $\frac{1}{16}$ lb.   1 lb. = _____ T.   _____ T. = 1 lb.

    1 lb. = **16** oz.

    $\frac{1}{16}$ lb. = 1 oz.

4. _____ lb. = 1 oz. $\frac{1}{2,000}$ T. = _____ lb. $\frac{1}{16}$ lb. = _____ oz.

Solve.

5. A package of chicken weighs 16 ounces. How many pounds are in 16 ounces?

   Answer _____

6. A truck carries a 1-ton load. How many pounds are in 1 ton?

   Answer _____

7. Bernice's baby son has gained 1 pound since he was born. How many ounces has her son gained since he was born?

   Answer _____

8. Tran's new compact car weighs 2,000 pounds. How many tons are in 2,000 pounds?

   Answer _____

STECK-VAUGHN
Mathematics Skill Book
Measurement and Geometry

Contents

Customary Measurement	2–10
Mixed Measurements	11–13
Checking Up	14
Adding and Subtracting Measurements	15–16
Multiplying and Dividing Measurements	17–18
Checking Up	19
Metric Measurements	20–23
Checking Up	24
Lines and Angles	25–28
Triangles	29–32
Checking Up	33
Polygons	34–35
Perimeter and Area	36–38
Circles	39
Volume	40
Checking Up	41
Coordinate Geometry	42–43
Progress Review	44–45
Answer Key	46–48

Introduction

Measurement and Geometry Mathematics Skill Book is designed to enable you to work on your own toward mastery of the fundamental concepts of customary and metric measurement as well as basic geometric shapes and formulas. The pages in this book combine the advantages of a textbook and a workbook by first showing you how certain types of problems should be solved and then providing similar practice exercises.

Mastery of concepts presented in *Measurement and Geometry Mathematics Skill Book* is aided by clear explanations and numerous examples. You should not treat some of the skill pages, especially those at the beginning of each content area, as being too elementary. These skills must be mastered before you can move on to more advanced exercises.

You can use the answers provided on pages 46–48 to check your own work. You should correct any errors before beginning work on the next skill page. Use the progress test on pages 44–45 to find out how well you have mastered the concepts in this book.

Copyright by Aztec Software, LLC.

All rights reserved. No part of this work may be reproduced or transmitted in any form or by any means, electronic or mechanical, including photocopying or recording, or by any information storage or retrieval system, without the prior written permission of the copyright owner, unless such copying is expressly permitted by federal copyright law. Requests for permission to make copies of any part of the work should be addressed to permissions@aztecsoftware.com or Aztec Software, LLC, 461 Headquarters Plaza, 2nd Floor, Morristown, NJ 07960.

ISBN 978-1-954456-33-4

1 2 3 4 5 6 7 8 9 10   PX2050   30 29 28 27 26 25 24 23

Customary Measures of Length

The table lists common customary units of measurement for length. The table shows how inches, feet, yards, and miles are related to each other. These relationships make it possible to change from one unit to another.

Measures of Length
1 foot (ft. or ') = 12 inches (in. or ")
1 yard (yd.) = 36 in.
1 yd. = 3 ft.
1 mile (mi.) = 5,280 ft.
1 mi. = 1,760 yd.

1 yd. = _____ in.   _____ yd. = 1 in.

To find an equivalent whole unit, use the table.

1 yd. = **36** in. and **36** in. = 1 yd.

To find an equivalent fractional unit, divide.

1 yd. = 36 in.

$\frac{1 \text{ yd.}}{36} = \frac{36 \text{ in.}}{36}$

$\frac{1}{36}$ yd. = 1 in. and 1 in. = $\frac{1}{36}$ yd.

Find the following equivalent whole units.

1. 1 ft. = __12__ in.   _____ in. = 1 ft.   _____ ft. = 1 yd.

2. _____ yd. = 36 in.   36 in. = _____ yd.   12 in. = _____ ft.

3. 1 mi. = _____ ft.   _____ ft. = 1 mi.   _____ yd. = 1 mi.

4. 5,280 ft. = _____ mi.   _____ mi. = 1,760 yd.   1,760 yd. = _____ mi.

Find the following equivalent fractional units.

5. $\frac{1}{12}$ ft. = 1 in.   _____ yd. = 1 ft.   1 in. = _____ ft.
 1 ft. = 12 in.
 $\frac{1}{12}$ ft. = 1 in.

6. _____ mi. = 1 ft.   _____ mi. = 1 yd.   1 ft. = _____ mi.

7. 1 ft. = _____ yd.   1 yd. = _____ mi.   1 in. = _____ yd.

Solve.

8. A piece of fabric is 1 foot long. What part of a yard is 1 foot?

   Answer _____

9. A hiking path is 5,280 feet long. How many miles long is the path?

   Answer _____

Customary Measures of Weight

To change a large unit, such as pounds, to a smaller unit, such as ounces, you multiply.

To change a small unit, such as ounces, to a larger unit, such as pounds, you divide. Reduce fractions to lowest terms.

$2\frac{1}{4}$ lb. = _____ oz.

20 oz. = _____ lb.

To change to a smaller unit, multiply.

1 lb. = 16 oz.

$2\frac{1}{4} \times 16 = \frac{9}{4} \times \frac{16}{1} = 36 \text{ oz.}$

To change to a larger unit, divide. Reduce if possible.

1 lb. = 16 oz.

$20 \div 16 = 1\frac{4}{16} = 1\frac{1}{4} \text{ lb.}$

Change each measurement to the smaller unit.

1. 6 T. = __12,000__ lb.
   1 T. = 2,000 lb.
   6 × 2,000 = 12,000 lb.

   $8\frac{1}{4}$ lb. = _____ oz.

   $\frac{1}{2}$ lb. = _____ oz.

2. $4\frac{1}{4}$ lb. = _____ oz.

   5 T. = _____ lb.

   $\frac{1}{4}$ T. = _____ lb.

3. 2 lb. = _____ oz.

   $\frac{3}{4}$ lb. = _____ oz.

   $3\frac{1}{4}$ T. = _____ lb.

Change each measurement to the larger unit. Reduce fractions if possible.

4. 40 oz. = __$2\frac{1}{2}$__ lb.
   1 lb. = 16 oz.
   $40 \div 16 = 2\frac{8}{16} = 2\frac{1}{2}$ lb.

   3 oz. = _____ lb.

   5,000 lb. = _____ T.

5. 32 oz. = _____ lb.

   1,000 lb. = _____ T.

   100 lb. = _____ T.

6. 1,500 lb. = _____ T.

   2 oz. = _____ lb.

   17,500 lb. = _____ T.

Solve.

7. Monte bought 18 ounces of ground turkey. How many pounds are in 18 ounces?

   Answer _____

8. A train shipment weighs $12\frac{1}{2}$ tons. How many pounds does the shipment weigh?

   Answer _____

Customary Measures of Capacity

The table lists common customary units of measurement for capacity. The table shows how fluid ounces, cups, pints, quarts, and gallons are related to each other. These relationships make it possible to change from one unit to another.

Measures of Capacity

1 cup (c.) = 8 fluid ounces (fl. oz.)
1 pint (pt.) = 2 c.
1 quart (qt.) = 4 c.
1 qt. = 2 pt.
1 gallon (gal.) = 4 qt.

1 pt. = _____ c.   _____ pt. = 1 c.

To find an equivalent whole unit, use the table.

1 pt. = 2 c. and 2 c. = 1 pt.

To find an equivalent fractional unit, divide.

1 pt. = 2 c.

$\frac{1\ pt.}{2} = \frac{2\ c.}{2}$

$\frac{1}{2}$ pt. = 1 c. and 1 c. = $\frac{1}{2}$ pt.

Find the following equivalent whole units.

1. 1 c. = __8__ fl. oz.   _____ fl. oz. = 1 c.   2 c. = _____ pt.

2. 1 qt. = _____ c.   _____ qt. = 2 pt.   2 pt. = _____ qt.

3. _____ c. = 8 fl. oz.   _____ qt. = 4 c.   1 gal. = _____ qt.

4. 4 c. = _____ qt.   1 qt. = _____ pt.   4 qt. = _____ gal.

Find the following equivalent fractional units.

5. __$\frac{1}{8}$__ c. = 1 fl. oz.   _____ gal. = 1 qt.   1 c. = _____ qt.
   1 c. = 8 fl. oz.
   $\frac{1}{8}$ c. = 1 fl. oz.

6. _____ qt. = 1 c.   _____ qt. = 1 pt.   1 fl. oz. = _____ c.

7. 1 pt. = _____ qt.   1 qt. = _____ gal.   1 c. = _____ pt.

Solve.

8. A recipe calls for 8 fluid ounces of milk. How many cups of milk does the recipe call for?

   Answer _____

9. Josie's car used $\frac{1}{4}$ gallon of oil. How many quarts of oil did the car use?

   Answer _____

Customary Measures of Capacity

To change a large unit, such as quarts, to a smaller unit, such as cups, you multiply.

To change a small unit, such as cups, to a larger unit, such as quarts, you divide. Reduce fractions to lowest terms.

$1\frac{1}{2}$ qt. = _____ c.

> To change to a smaller unit, multiply.
>
> 1 qt. = 4 c.
>
> $1\frac{1}{2} \times 4 = \frac{3}{2} \times \frac{4}{1} = 6$ c.

10 c. = _____ qt.

> To change to a larger unit, divide. Reduce if possible.
>
> 1 qt. = 4 c.
>
> $10 \div 4 = 2\frac{2}{4} = 2\frac{1}{2}$ qt.

Change each measurement to the smaller unit.

1. $8\frac{1}{2}$ pt. = __17__ c.
  1 pt. = 2 c.
  $8\frac{1}{2} \times 2 = \frac{17}{2} \times \frac{2}{1} = 17$ c.

  $2\frac{1}{2}$ gal. = _____ qt.

  5 c. = _____ fl. oz.

2. $4\frac{1}{2}$ qt. = _____ c.

  $\frac{1}{2}$ pt. = _____ c.

  $3\frac{1}{2}$ c. = _____ fl. oz.

3. 5 gal. = _____ qt.

  $\frac{3}{4}$ gal. = _____ qt.

  2 pt. = _____ c.

Change each measurement to the larger unit. Reduce fractions if possible.

4. 6 c. = $1\frac{1}{2}$ qt.
  1 qt. = 4 c.
  $6 \div 4 = 1\frac{2}{4} = 1\frac{1}{2}$ qt.

  40 qt. = _____ gal.

  16 c. = _____ pt.

5. 3 pt. = _____ qt.

  6 pt. = _____ qt.

  4 fl. oz. = _____ c.

6. 5 c. = _____ pt.

  7 c. = _____ qt.

  12 fl. oz. = _____ c.

Solve.

7. After jogging, John drank 20 fluid ounces of water. How many cups of water did John drink?

   Answer _____

8. Barbara canned 12 quarts of green beans. How many pints of green beans did Barbara can?

   Answer _____

Customary Measures of Time

The table lists common customary units of measurement for time. The table shows how seconds, minutes, hours, days, weeks, months, and years are related to each other. These relationships make it possible to change from one unit to another.

Measures of Time

1 minute (min.) = 60 seconds (sec.)
1 hour (hr.) = 60 min.
1 day = 24 hr.
1 week (wk.) = 7 days
1 year (yr.) = 52 wk.
1 yr. = 12 months (mo.)

1 hr. = _____ min.

_____ hr. = 1 min.

To find an equivalent whole unit, use the table.

1 hr. = **60** min. and **60** min. = 1 hr.

To find an equivalent fractional unit, divide.

1 hr. = 60 min.

$\frac{1}{60}$ hr. = $\frac{60}{60}$ min.

$\frac{1}{60}$ hr. = 1 min. and 1 min. = $\frac{1}{60}$ hr.

Find the following equivalent whole units.

1. 1 min. = __60__ sec.   _____ sec. = 1 min.   1 day = _____ hr.

2. 1 yr. = _____ wk.   _____ wk. = 1 yr.   _____ mo. = 1 yr.

3. _____ wk. = 7 days   _____ yr. = 12 mo.   12 mo. = _____ yr.

4. _____ min. = 60 sec.   60 min. = _____ hr.   24 hr. = _____ day

Find the following equivalent fractional units.

5. $\frac{1}{24}$ day = 1 hr.   _____ wk. = 1 day   1 mo. = _____ yr.

   1 day = 24 hr.

   $\frac{1}{24}$ day = 1 hr.

6. _____ yr. = 1 wk.   _____ yr. = 1 mo.   1 day = _____ wk.

Solve.

7. Pat's speech was 60 minutes long. How many hours long was Pat's speech?

   Answer _____

8. Dave's job allows him to take vacation 1 month every year. What part of a year does Dave take off for vacation?

   Answer _____

Customary Measures of Time

To change a large unit, such as weeks, to a smaller unit, such as days, you multiply.

To change a small unit, such as days, to a larger unit, such as weeks, you divide. Reduce fractions to lowest terms.

3 wk. = _____ days

To change to a smaller unit, multiply. 1 wk. = 7 days 3 × 7 = 21 days

30 days = _____ wk.

To change to a larger unit, divide. Reduce if possible. 1 wk. = 7 days 30 ÷ 7 = $4\frac{2}{7}$ wk.

Change each measurement to the smaller unit.

1. 8 hr. = __480__ min.
   1 hr. = 60 min.
   8 × 60 = 480

   $8\frac{1}{2}$ days = _____ hr.

   $2\frac{1}{2}$ yr. = _____ mo.

2. $4\frac{1}{4}$ min. = _____ sec.

   3 yr. = _____ wk.

   4 days = _____ hr.

3. 15 wk. = _____ days

   6 hr. = _____ min.

   5 min. = _____ sec.

Change each measurement to the larger unit. Reduce fractions if possible.

4. 80 min. = __$1\frac{1}{3}$__ hr.
   1 hr. = 60 min.
   80 ÷ 60 = $1\frac{20}{60} = 1\frac{1}{3}$

   16 mo. = _____ yr.

   90 sec. = _____ min.

5. 48 mo. = _____ yr.

   75 min. = _____ hr.

   8 hr. = _____ day

6. 104 wk. = _____ yr.

   3 mo. = _____ yr.

   48 hr. = _____ days

Solve.

7. Mary is 22 months younger than her sister. Change 22 months to years.

   Answer _____

8. The clock showed there were 4 minutes left in the basketball game. How many seconds were left in the game?

   Answer _____

Comparing Measurements

To compare measurements, make sure that the units are the same. You may need to change the unit of one of the measurements. Usually it is easier to change a large unit to a smaller unit. Then compare the numbers.

Compare 18 ft. to 4 yd.

Change 4 yd. to ft.	Compare.
4 yd. = 12 ft.	18 ft. > 12 ft., so 18 ft. > 4 yd.

Compare the measurements. Write >, <, or =.

1. 8 in. [<] 1 ft.
   1 ft. = 12 in.
   8 in. < 12 in.

   3 c. ☐ 1 qt.

   22 oz. ☐ 1 lb.

2. 72 hr. ☐ 3 days

   5 yd. ☐ 20 ft.

   2 T. ☐ 1,750 lb.

3. 150 min. ☐ 2 hr.

   $2\frac{1}{2}$ gal. ☐ 5 qt.

   5 mi. ☐ 15,840 ft.

4. 8 wk. ☐ 60 days

   $3\frac{1}{4}$ lb. ☐ 50 oz.

   $6\frac{1}{2}$ pt. ☐ 3 qt.

5. 70 in. ☐ $1\frac{1}{3}$ yd.

   16 fl. oz. ☐ 2 c.

   150 sec. ☐ 3 min.

6. 3 lb. ☐ 48 oz.

   $\frac{1}{2}$ mi. ☐ 3,000 ft.

   6 qt. ☐ 2 gal.

7. $2\frac{1}{2}$ hr. ☐ 150 min.

   32 oz. ☐ $1\frac{1}{2}$ lb.

   $\frac{1}{2}$ gal. ☐ 3 qt.

Solve.

8. Anna needs $1\frac{1}{2}$ yards of rope to hang a bird house. She has a piece of rope that is 30 inches long. Does she have enough rope to hang the bird house?

   Answer _____

9. Norman walked for 90 minutes on Monday. On Wednesday, he walked for 2 hours. Did he walk longer on Monday or Wednesday?

   Answer _____

Mixed Measurements

Mixed measurements contain more than one unit such as 2 feet 6 inches. The answer given in both units is the simplified answer.

A measurement containing a fraction or a decimal can be changed to a mixed measurement. For example, $2\frac{1}{2}$ feet and 2.5 feet are both equal to 2 feet 6 inches.

$3\frac{1}{4}$ hr. = _____ hr. _____ min.

> Change $\frac{1}{4}$ hr. to min.
> $\frac{1}{4}$ hr. = $\frac{1}{4}$ hr. × 60 min. = 15 min.
> $3\frac{1}{4}$ hr. = 3 hr. 15 min.

1.5 c. = _____ c. _____ fl. oz.

> Change 0.5 c. to fl. oz.
> 0.5 c. = .5 c. × 8 fl. oz. = 4 fl. oz.
> 1.5 c. = 1 c. 4 fl. oz.

Change each measurement to the units given.

1. $1\frac{1}{3}$ yd. = __1__ yd. __1__ ft.
   $\frac{1}{3}$ yd. = $\frac{1}{3}$ yd. × 3 ft. = 1 ft.

   $2\frac{1}{4}$ lb. = _____ lb. _____ oz.

2. $4\frac{1}{2}$ gal. = _____ gal. _____ qt.

   3.5 hr. = _____ hr. _____ min.

3. $10\frac{1}{3}$ ft. = _____ ft. _____ in.

   2.5 qt. = _____ qt. _____ pt.

4. $5\frac{3}{4}$ yr. = _____ yr. _____ mo.

   1.1 T. = _____ T. _____ lb.

5. 4.5 pt. = _____ pt. _____ c.

   2.2 mi. = _____ mi. _____ ft.

6. 2.25 lb. = _____ lb. _____ oz.

   $6\frac{1}{3}$ days = _____ days _____ hr.

Solve.

7. Joshua runs the mile in $5\frac{3}{4}$ minutes. Write $5\frac{3}{4}$ minutes as a mixed measurement.

   Answer _____

8. Mack bought some fencing that is $2\frac{1}{2}$ feet high. What is the height of the fencing in feet and inches?

   Answer _____

Mixed Measurements

To change a measurement to mixed units, divide. The whole number in the answer is the number of larger units, the remainder is the number of smaller units.

14 in. = _____ ft. _____ in.

> Divide.
> 1 ft. = 12 in.
> 14 ÷ 12 = 1 R 2
> 14 in. = 1 ft. 2 in.

Change each measurement to the units given.

1. 39 in. = __1__ yd. __3__ in.
   39 ÷ 36 = 1 R 3

   100 hr. = _____ days _____ hr.

2. 15 c. = _____ pt. _____ c.

   40 oz. = _____ lb. _____ oz.

3. 2,112 yd. = _____ mi. _____ yd.

   11 qt. = _____ gal. _____ qt.

4. 195 min. = _____ hr. _____ min.

   3,050 lb. = _____ T. _____ lb.

5. 17 pt. = _____ qt. _____ pt.

   50 mo. = _____ yr. _____ mo.

6. 22 oz. = _____ lb. _____ oz.

   19 ft. = _____ yd. _____ ft.

7. 78 wk. = _____ yr. _____ wk.

   16,368 ft. = _____ mi. _____ ft.

8. 5,200 lb. = _____ T. _____ lb.

   30 fl. oz. = _____ c. _____ fl. oz.

9. 200 sec. = _____ min. _____ sec.

   16 ft. = _____ yd. _____ ft.

Solve.

10. Ann is 70 inches tall. What is her height in feet and inches?

    Answer_____

11. Mark is 18 months old. What is his age in years and months?

    Answer_____

Mixed Measurements

To change a mixed measurement to the smaller unit, change the larger unit to the smaller unit. Then add them.

To change a mixed measurement to the larger unit, change the smaller unit to the larger unit. Then add. The answer will be a mixed number or decimal.

2 yd. 2 ft. = _____ ft.

> Change 2 yd. to ft.
> 2 yd. = 6 ft.
> Add.
> 6 ft. + 2 ft. = 8 ft.

2 yd. 2 ft. = _____ yd.

> Change 2 ft. to yd.
> 2 ft. = $\frac{2}{3}$ yd.
> Add.
> 2 yd. + $\frac{2}{3}$ yd. = $2\frac{2}{3}$ yd.

Change each measurement to the unit given.

1. 3 qt. 1 pt. = __7__ pt.   5 lb. 2 oz. = _____ lb.   2 hr. 40 min. = _____ min.
   3 qt. = 6 pt.
   6 + 1 = 7

2. 6 ft. 3 in. = _____ ft.   1 pt. 1 c. = _____ c.   1 T. 500 lb. = _____ T.

3. 5 wk. 3 days = _____ days   6 mi. 2,640 ft. = _____ mi.   2 gal. 3 qt. = _____ qt.

4. 1 lb. 12 oz. = _____ lb.   3 days 15 hr. = _____ hr.   7 yd. 1 ft. = _____ yd.

5. 3 c. 6 fl. oz. = _____ fl. oz.   2 T. 200 lb. = _____ lb.   3 min. 10 sec. = _____ min.

6. 8 ft. 2 in. = _____ in.   5 qt. 1 pt. = _____ qt.   3 lb. 4 oz. = _____ oz.

Solve.

7. Rubio mailed a package of car parts that weighed 12 pounds 8 ounces. What was the total weight of the package in ounces?

   Answer _____

8. Martha bought 6 yards 2 feet of curtain material. Write 6 yards 2 feet as yards.

   Answer _____

Checking Up

Change each measurement. Reduce fractions if possible.

1. 12 in. = _____ ft.   1 yd. = _____ ft.   2,640 ft. = _____ mi.

2. $5\frac{1}{2}$ ft. = _____ in. $3\frac{1}{4}$ mi. = _____ yd.   16 oz. = _____ lb.

3. $\frac{1}{4}$ lb. = _____ oz.   3 lb. = _____ oz. $1\frac{1}{2}$ gal. = _____ qt.

4. 1 qt. = _____ c. $\frac{1}{2}$ gal. = _____ qt.   1 c. = _____ pt.

5. 10 fl. oz. = _____ c.   6 pt. = _____ qt.   60 min. = _____ hr.

6. $\frac{1}{2}$ yr. = _____ wk.   9 wk. = _____ days $1\frac{1}{4}$ hr. = _____ min.

Compare the measurements. Write >, <, or =.

7. 20 in. ☐ $1\frac{1}{2}$ ft.   2 hr. ☐ 120 min.   50 oz. ☐ $3\frac{1}{2}$ lb.

Change each measurement to the units given.

8. $3\frac{1}{2}$ c. = _____ c. _____ fl. oz.   7.25 lb. = _____ lb. _____ oz.

9. 2.5 yd. = _____ yd. _____ in. $1\frac{1}{4}$ hr. = _____ hr. _____ min.

10. 80 in. = _____ ft. _____ in.   14 mo. = _____ yr. _____ mo.

11. 9,000 lb. = _____ T. _____ lb.   15 qt. = _____ gal. _____ qt.

12. 5 pt. 1 c. = _____ c.   5 lb. 3 oz. = _____ oz.

13. 5 days 12 hr. = _____ hr.   2 ft. 4 in. = _____ in.

Solve.

14. A cooked ham on sale weighs 88 ounces. What is the weight of the ham in pounds and ounces?

    Answer_____

15. A grocery store has two brands of orange juice on sale for the same price. Tasty brand is sold in 64-ounce bottles. Sun City brand is sold in 2 quart 4 ounce-bottles. Which brand has more orange juice for the sale price?

    Answer_____

Adding Measurements

When adding measurements, add only like units. Simplify answers when possible.

Add 2 lb. 10 oz. + 3 lb. 8 oz.

Set up the problem vertically and add.	Change 18 oz. to 1 lb. 2 oz.
2 lb. 10 oz. + 3 lb. 8 oz. ——————— 5 lb. 18 oz.	Add and simplify. 5 lb. + 1 lb. 2 oz. = 6 lb. 2 oz.

Add. Simplify if possible.

1.   2 c. 5 fl. oz.   3 yd. 1 ft.   5 days 12 hr.
   + 4 c. 5 fl. oz.   + 2 yd. 2 ft.   + 3 days 12 hr.
   ————————————
   6 c. 10 fl. oz. = 7 c. 2 fl. oz.

2.   1 T. 1,000 lb.   2 qt. 1 c.   5 mi. 100 yd.
   + 2 T.   500 lb.   + 1 qt. 1 c.   + 4 mi. 900 yd.

3.   16 hr. 50 min.   5 lb. 19 oz.   9 gal. 2 qt.
   + 3 hr. 40 min.   + 6 lb. 21 oz.   + 12 gal. 5 qt.

4. 1 ft. 3 in. + 1 ft. 9 in. =   18 min. 20 sec. + 17 min. 45 sec. =

5. 4 T. 1,500 lb. + 2 T. 500 lb. =   1 gal. 2 qt. + 3 gal. 3 qt. =

6. 1 yd. 1 ft. + 2 yd. 2 ft. =   5 lb. 4 oz. + 12 lb. 14 oz. =

Solve.

7. Eleanor bought two packages of chicken. One package weighed 3 pounds 6 ounces and the other package weighed 2 pounds 10 ounces. How many pounds of chicken did she buy all together?

   Answer _____

8. Thomas worked for 7 hours 30 minutes on Monday and for 6 hours 50 minutes on Tuesday. How long did he work on Monday and Tuesday?

   Answer _____

Subtracting Measurements

When subtracting measurements, subtract only like units. Sometimes you will need to borrow. Be sure to change the borrowed number to the correct unit before you subtract.

Subtract 1 hr. 10 min. − 30 min.

Set up the problem.	Borrow and subtract.

1 hr. 10 min.
−   30 min.
	0 70
	   X̸ hr. 1̸0̸ min.
	− 30 min.
	              40 min.

Subtract.

1.   0 22
   X̸ ft. 1̸0̸ in.
−   12 in.
              10 in.

    1 qt. 1 pt.
−   3 pt.

    1 lb. 5 oz.
−   12 oz.

2.   2 min. 30 sec.
−   45 sec.

    4 yd. 2 ft.
−   5 ft.

    5 pt. 1 c.
−   3 c.

3.   12 yr. 4 mo.
−   1 yr. 10 mo.

    8 ft. 7 in.
− 3 ft. 10 in.

    10 gal. 2 qt.
− 5 gal. 3 qt.

4. 2 T. 1,000 lb. − 1,500 lb. =

    5 days 12 hr. − 16 hr. =

5. 3 mi. 1,000 ft. − 1 mi. 2,000 ft. =

    9 yd. 2 ft. − 2 yd. 3 ft. =

Solve.

6. A window is 3 feet 6 inches tall and 2 feet 10 inches wide. How much taller is the window than it is wide?

   Answer _____

7. William bought 2 gallons of cider for a party. He and his guests drank 1 gallon 2 quarts. How much cider was left over after the party?

   Answer _____

Multiplying Measurements

When multiplying measurements, multiply each unit separately.
Simplify if possible.

Multiply 4 pt. 1 c. × 5

Set up the problem and multiply.	Change 5 c. to 2 pt. 1 c.
4 pt. 1 c. × 5 20 pt. 5 c.	Add and simplify. 20 pt. + 2 pt. 1 c. = 22 pt. 1 c.

Multiply. Simplify if possible.

1.   3 lb. 4 oz.   10 min. 30 sec.   1 ft. 6 in.
    ×   4   ×   6   ×   9
    12 lb. 16 oz. = 13 lb.

2.   1 c. 3 fl. oz.   1 day 19 hr.   2 ft. 8 in.
    ×   3   ×   2   ×   5

3.   6 qt.   20 hr.   2.5 yr.
    ×   7   ×   2   ×   6

4. 1 gal. 1 qt. × 7 =   3 T. 1,000 lb. × 4 =   3.2 mi. × 5 =

5. 12 oz. × 16 =   3 days × 10 =   6 yd. × 12 =

6. $5\frac{1}{2}$ pt. × 8 = $1\frac{1}{2}$ ft. × 6 = $2\frac{1}{4}$ T. × 4 =

Solve.

7. A square box is $1\frac{1}{2}$ feet long on each side. The perimeter of a square is four times the length of one side. What is the perimeter of the box?

    Answer _____

8. It takes Matti 45 minutes to embroider one pillowcase. How long will it take her to embroider 6 pillowcases?

    Answer _____

Dividing Measurements

When dividing measurements, divide into the larger unit first. If there is a remainder, change the remainder to the smaller unit and add. Then divide again.

Divide 3 ft. 4 in. ÷ 2

Set up the problem and divide.	Change 1 ft. to 12 in. Add and divide again.

1 ft.
2)3 ft.   4 in.
 − 2
   1 ft.
	1 ft. 8 in.
	2)3 ft. 4 in.
	 − 2
	   1 ft. = + 12 in.
	             16 in.
	           − 16
	               0

Divide.

1.   1 c.   7 fl. oz.
   2)3 c.   6 fl. oz.
    − 2
      1 c. = + 8 fl. oz.
              14 fl. oz.
            − 14
               0

               4)5 lb. 4 oz.   6)7 hr. 30 min.

2. 3)5 yd. 6 in.   5)6 qt. 3 pt.   2)4 T. 500 lb.

3. 10 days 12 hr. ÷ 4 =   8 mi. 1,760 ft. ÷ 4 =   11 gal. 1 qt. ÷ 5 =

Solve.

4. A 5-ton load of wood was divided equally among 4 trucks. How much wood was on each truck?

   Answer _____

5. Carlos needs to cut shelving that is 7 feet 9 inches long into 3 equal pieces. How long will each of the three pieces of shelving be?

   Answer _____

Checking Up

Add, subtract, multiply, or divide. Simplify if possible.

1.   2 lb. 4 oz.   5 yd. 1 ft.   2 pt. 1 c.
    + 9 lb. 12 oz.   + 3 yd. 2 ft.   + 5 pt. 1 c.

2. 3 yr. 4 mo. + 9 yr. 10 mo. =   5 gal. 1 qt. + 1 gal. 3 qt. =

3.   1 ft. 1 in.   4 gal. 1 qt.   10 wk. 3 days
   −   6 in.   − 1 gal. 3 qt.   − 7 wk. 5 days

4. 5 T. 500 lb. − 1,000 lb. =   4 yd. 9 in. − 1 yd. 10 in. =

5.   3 qt. 1 c.   5 days 3 hr.   1 mi. 1,320 ft.
   ×   4   ×   8   ×   5

6. 6 yd. 1 ft. × 6 =   3 gal. 1 qt. × 3 =   1 mi. 440 yd. × 4 =

7. 2)2 hr. 30 min.   4)4 T. 1,000 lb.   3)7 pt. 1 c.

8. 10 mi. 2,640 yd. ÷ 5 =   6 lb. 6 oz. ÷ 3 =   1 hr. 20 min. ÷ 4 =

Solve.

9. Lorenzo exercises 3 times a week for 1 hour and 30 minutes each time. What is the total amount of time Lorenzo exercises each week?

    Answer _____

10. Pete's baby weighed 16 pounds 4 ounces last month. Now the baby weighs 17 pounds 1 ounce. How much weight has the baby gained since last month?

    Answer _____

19

Metric Length, Weight, and Capacity

The metric system of measurement is based on the decimal system. To change from a large metric unit to a smaller metric unit, count the number of steps from one unit to the other. Move the decimal point to the right one place for each step.

To compare metric measures, change to like units. Then compare.

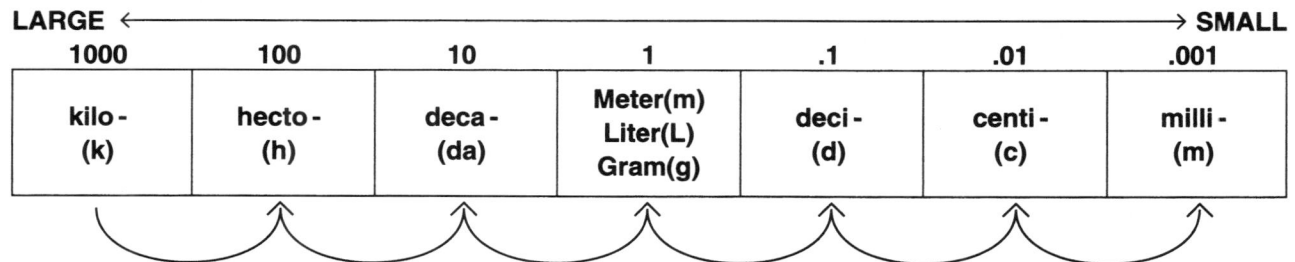

2.1 m = _____ cm

Count 2 steps from meter to centimeter. Move the decimal point 2 places to the right.
2.10
2.1 m = 210 cm

Compare 5 m to 5 cm.

Change 5 m to cm.
5 m = 500 cm
500 cm > 5 cm, so 5 m > 5 cm

Change each measurement.

1. 3.4 kL = **34,000** dL   1.39 hg = _____ g   15.7 m = _____ mm
   34000

2. 270 cL = _____ mL   100 g = _____ dg   3 dam = _____ cm

3. 0.345 L = _____ dL   0.5 hm = _____ mm   0.002 kg = _____ g

Change the large unit to the smaller unit. Then compare. Write >, <, or =.

4. 150 m **<** 15 km   3.2 cL ☐ 320 dL   5 mg ☐ 0.5 cg
   15 km = 1500 m

5. 1 km ☐ 100 m   4.5 L ☐ 45 mL   7 g ☐ 700 mg

Solve.

6. How many milliliters does a 1-liter bottle of soda contain?

   Answer _____

7. Which is longer, a 3.5-kilometer or a 350-meter nature trail?

   Answer _____

20

Metric Length, Weight, and Capacity

To change from a small metric unit to a larger metric unit, count the number of steps from one unit to the other. Move the decimal point to the left one place for each step.

To compare metric measures, change to like units. Then compare.

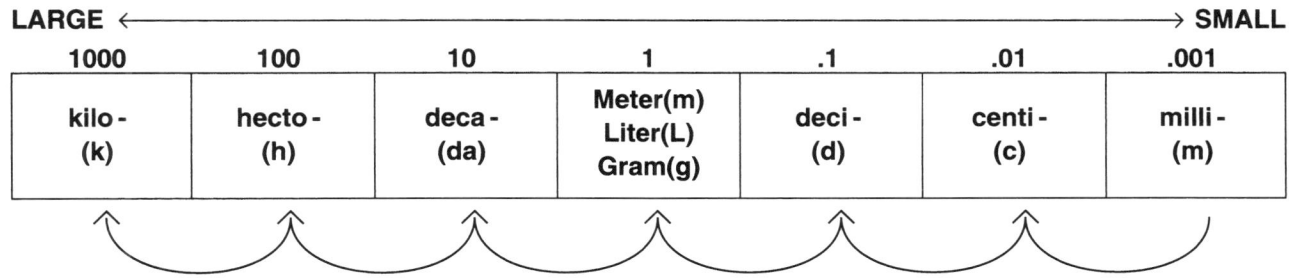

41 cg = _____ dag

Count 3 steps from centigram to decagram. Move the decimal point 3 places to the left.
.041
41 cg = 0.041 dag

Compare 900 g to 9 kg.

Change 900 g to kg.
900 g = 0.9 kg
0.9 kg < 9 kg, so 900 g < 9 kg

Change each measurement.

1. 10,000 L = __10__ kL   3,000 cm = _____ m   1,115 mg = _____ cg
   10000

2. 300 cL = _____ daL   1,500 m = _____ km   40 mg = _____ g

3. 52,000 cL = _____ L   360 mm = _____ cm   6,000 g = _____ kg

Change the small unit to the larger unit. Then compare. Write >, <, or =.

4. 4,500 mL [<] 45 L   1.5 km ☐ 150 cm   10,000 mg ☐ 1 dag
   4500 mL = 4.5 L

5. 5 L ☐ 50 mL   18 dm ☐ 1.8 m   0.7 kg ☐ 7 g

Solve.

6. A bag of potatoes weighs 5,000 grams. How many kilograms is 5,000 grams?

   Answer _____

7. Which bottle contains more water, a 1.5-liter bottle or a 150-milliliter bottle of water?

   Answer _____

21

Adding and Subtracting Metric Measurements

When you add or subtract metric units, add or subtract only like units.

Add 3,000 g + 20 kg = _____ kg

| Change 3,000 g to kg. |
| 3000 g = 3 kg |
| Add. |
| 20 kg + 3 kg = 23 kg |

Subtract 8 L − 100 cL = _____ L

| Change 100 cL to L. |
| 100 cL = 1 L |
| Subtract. |
| 8 L − 1 L = 7 L |

Change to like units. Then add or subtract.

1. 400 mm + 3 cm = __43__ cm   500 cg − 40 mg = _____ cg   10 hL − 10 L = _____ L
   400 mm = 40 cm
   40 + 3 = 43 cm

2. 2 dm + 2 m = _____ dm   1,800 dg + 0.5 kg = _____ kg   50 L − 2,500 cL = _____ L

3. 15 m − 700 cm = _____ m   1 kg − 500 g = _____ kg   15 kL + 600 L = _____ kL

4. 5 hm + 40 dam = _____ hm   750 mL − 10 cL = _____ cL   100 mg + 80 dg = _____ dg

5. 0.6 m + 50 cm = _____ m   1.3 kg − 400 g = _____ g   500 mL − 2.5 cL = _____ cL

6. 10.7 g + 90 cg = _____ g   0.7 kL − 7L = _____ L   9.1 hm + 10 dam = _____ hm

7. 2.2 km − 200 m = _____ km   9.5 g − 300 mg = _____ g   20 cL + 3.8 L = _____ L

Solve.

8. One package of flower seeds weighs 200 milligrams. Another package weighs 4 grams. What is the total weight in grams of the two packages?

   Answer _____

9. A new ball of string contains 10 meters of string. If you use 30 centimeters, how many meters of string are left on the ball?

   Answer _____

Multiplying and Dividing Metric Measurements

When you multiply or divide metric measurements, follow the same steps as in multiplying and dividing decimals. Be sure to put the decimal point in the correct place in the answer.

Multiply 125 L × 13 = _____ kL

> Multiply.
>
> 125 L × 13 = 1,625 L
>
> Change to the unit given.
>
> 1625 L = 1.625 kL

Divide 0.96 m ÷ 6 = _____ cm

> Divide.
>
> 0.96 m ÷ 6 = 0.16 m
>
> Change to the unit given.
>
> 0.16 m = 16 cm

Multiply or divide. Change each answer to the unit given.

1. 350 g × 5 = __1.75__ kg
   350 g × 5 = 1,750 g
   1750 g = 1.75 kg

   0.8 L ÷ 20 = _____ cL

   62 cm × 7 = _____ m

2. 400 cg ÷ 10 = _____ mg

   9 kL ÷ 900 = _____ L

   5 m × 200 = _____ km

3. 7.2 dg × 30 = _____ dag

   3 hL ÷ 15 = _____ daL

   1 dm ÷ 5 = _____ cm

4. 4 mg × 12 = _____ g

   60 cL ÷ 2 = _____ mL

   9 mm × 24 = _____ cm

5. 110 hg × 8 = _____ kg

   70 mL × 45 = _____ L

   8 km ÷ 400 = _____ m

6. 3.7 g ÷ 20 = _____ cg

   26.3 L × 5 = _____ daL

   60 m × 30 = _____ km

7. 300 mg × 4 = _____ g

   200 mL ÷ 40 = _____ cL

   18.9 cm ÷ 3 = _____ mm

Solve.

8. One bottle contains 1.5 liters of cooking oil. How many kiloliters of cooking oil do 12 bottles contain?

   Answer _____

9. A 10-gram package of spice is divided into 4 jars the same size. How many milligrams of spice are in each jar?

   Answer _____

23

Checking Up

Change each measurement to the unit given.

1. 5.9 km = _____ m   9 L = _____ mL   0.06 kg = _____ mg

2. 100 cm = _____ mm   7.3 hL = _____ L   40 g = _____ cg

3. 3.1 m = _____ cm   2 L = _____ dL   8 hg = _____ g

4. 5,000 m = _____ km   300 mL = _____ L   60 cg = _____ dg

5. 880 cm = _____ m   100 L = _____ kL   93 g = _____ dag

6. 2,000 mm = _____ dm   500 dL = _____ hL   320 kg = _____ g

Compare. Write >, <, or =.

7. 20 m ☐ 2 km   500 cL ☐ 5 kL   160 cg ☐ 1.6 g

8. 3,500 mm ☐ 3.5 dm   6 L ☐ 0.6 hL   900,000 mg ☐ 0.9 kg

Add, subtract, multiply, or divide. Change each answer to the unit given.

9. 250 cm + 2 m = _____ m   15 L + 3,000 mL = _____ L   1.9 kg + 100 g = _____ kg

10. 6 m − 400 cm = _____ m   3 dL − 30 cL = _____ dL   8 dag − 5 g = _____ dag

11. 150 mm × 10 = _____ dm   7 hL × 20 = _____ kL   19 g × 100 = _____ kg

12. 4 m ÷ 10 = _____ dam   1,000 mL ÷ 5 = _____ L   20 kg ÷ 4 = _____ g

Solve.

13. Inez ran 6 times around a 500-meter track. How many kilometers did she run?

    Answer _____

14. How many grams are in a can of soup that weighs 0.524 kilograms?

    Answer _____

Lines and Angles

Lines and angles are named and labeled as shown in these examples. Study the examples.

 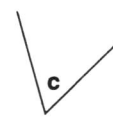  

The angle is named ∠B or ∠ABC. | **acute angle** ∠c < 90° | **right angle** ∠M = 90° | **obtuse angle** between 90° and 180°

 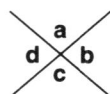 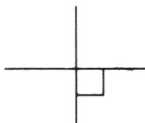 

straight angle 180° | **intersecting lines** | **perpendicular lines** | **parallel lines**

Label each angle or set of lines.

1.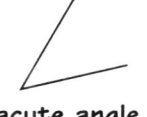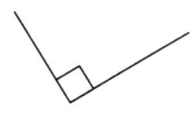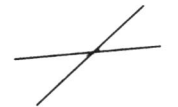

   acute angle

2.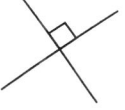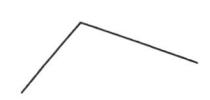

3.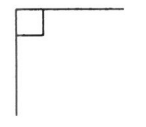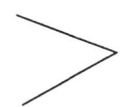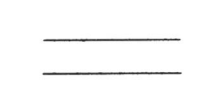

Write the name of each angle.

4.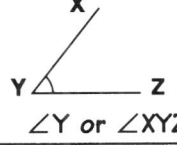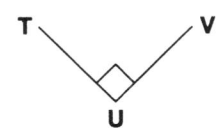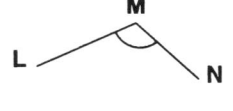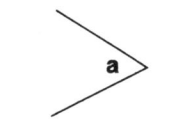

   ∠Y or ∠XYZ

Solve.

5. Third Street and the railroad tracks both run north to south, side-by-side. Third Street and the railroad tracks are (perpendicular, parallel, or intersecting) lines.

   Answer _____

6. Jill drove 2 blocks north on Third Street and turned due west on Miller Avenue. The angle formed at the corner of Third Street and Miller Avenue is a (straight, acute, or right) angle.

   Answer _____

25

Measuring Angles

A protractor is used to measure angles in degrees from 0° to 180°.

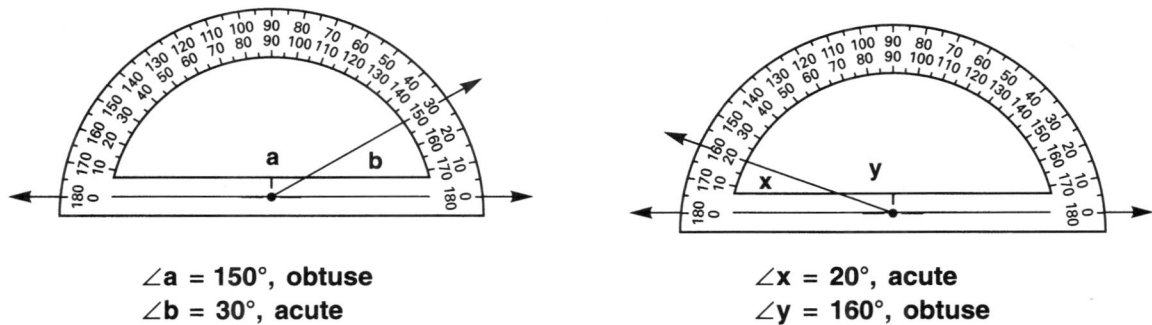

∠a = 150°, obtuse
∠b = 30°, acute

∠x = 20°, acute
∠y = 160°, obtuse

Find the measure of each angle. Identify each angle as acute, obtuse, or right.

1.

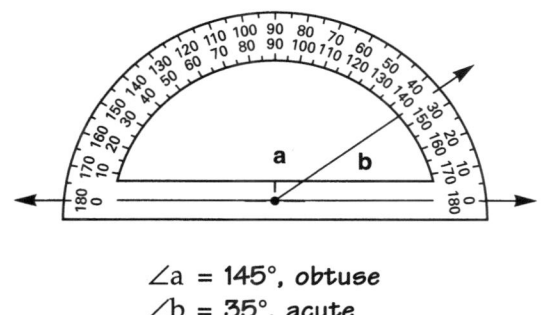

∠a = 145°, obtuse
∠b = 35°, acute

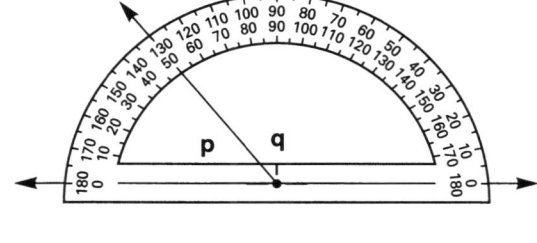

∠p =
∠q =

2.

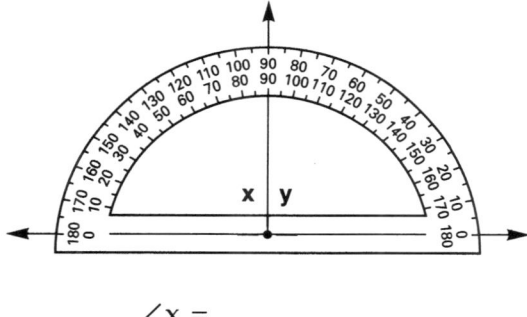

∠x =
∠y =

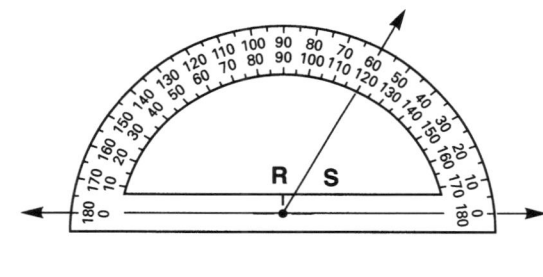

∠R =
∠S =

3.

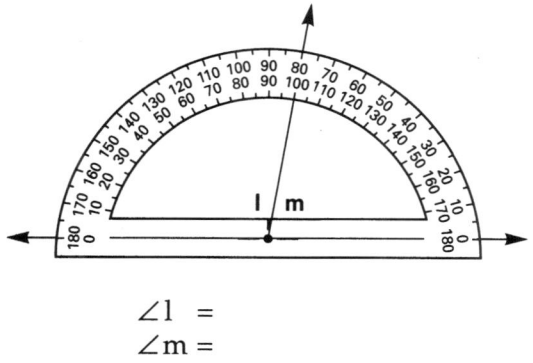

∠l =
∠m =

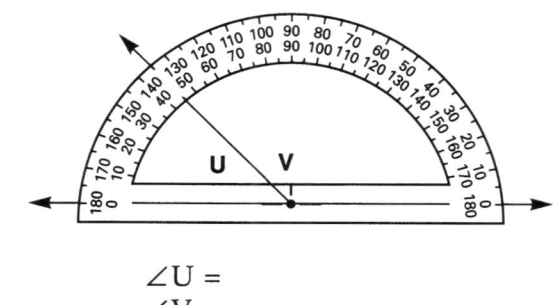

∠U =
∠V =

Complementary and Supplementary Angles

Two angles are called complementary if the sum of both the angles is 90°.

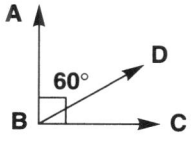

∠ABC = 90°
∠ABD = 60°
∠DBC = 90° − 60°
∠DBC = 30°

Two angles are called supplementary if the sum of both the angles is 180°.

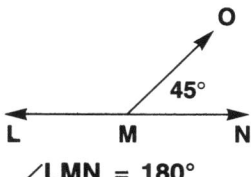

∠LMN = 180°
∠OMN = 45°
∠LMO = 180° − 45°
∠LMO = 135°

Find the measure of each unknown angle.

1.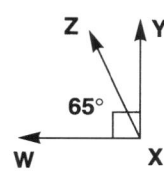

   ∠WXY = 90°
   ∠WXZ = 65°
   ∠ZXY = 90° − 65° = 25°

   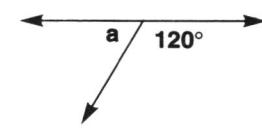

   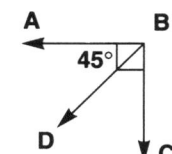

2.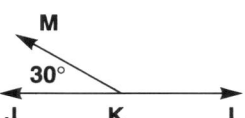

   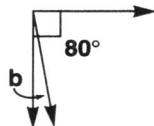

   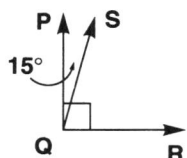

3.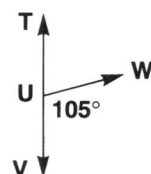

   (d, 30°)

   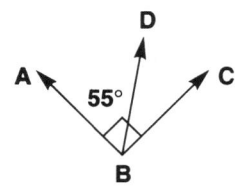

4.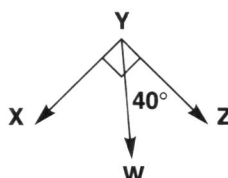

   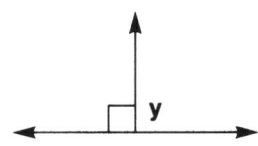

   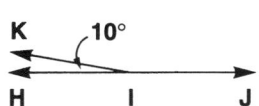

27

Vertical Angles and Transversals

When two straight lines cross, they form four angles. The opposite angles are called vertical angles.

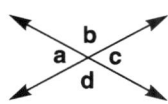

Vertical angles are equal.
∠a = ∠c, ∠b = ∠d

∠a + ∠b = 180°
∠c + ∠d = 180°

When two parallel lines are cut by a third line, a transversal, eight angles are formed.

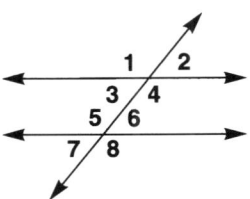

Corresponding angles are equal.
∠1 = ∠5, ∠2 = ∠6, ∠3 = ∠7, ∠4 = ∠8
Alternate interior angles are equal.
∠3 = ∠6, ∠4 = ∠5
Alternate exterior angles are equal.
∠1 = ∠8, ∠2 = ∠7

Use the information shown above to find the unknown angle measures.

1. ∠a = 40°
   ∠b = 180° − 40° = 140°
   ∠c = 40°
   ∠d = 140°

   ∠a =
   ∠b = 100°
   ∠c =
   ∠d =

   ∠a =
   ∠b =
   ∠c = 50°
   ∠d =

2. ∠a =
   ∠b =
   ∠c =
   ∠d = 110°

   ∠a = 35°
   ∠b =
   ∠c =
   ∠d =

   ∠a =
   ∠b = 107°
   ∠c =
   ∠d =

3. ∠1 = 95°
   ∠2 =
   ∠3 =
   ∠4 =
   ∠5 =
   ∠6 =
   ∠7 =
   ∠8 =

   ∠1 =
   ∠2 = 75°
   ∠3 =
   ∠4 =
   ∠5 =
   ∠6 =
   ∠7 =
   ∠8 =

   ∠1 =
   ∠2 =
   ∠3 = 88°
   ∠4 =
   ∠5 =
   ∠6 =
   ∠7 =
   ∠8 =

Solve.

4. Major Road is being built to cross Park Street and Main Street at a 60° angle. Find the measures of each unknown angle.

   ∠a =   ∠c =

   ∠d =   ∠e =

   ∠f =   ∠g =

   ∠h =

Triangles

A triangle has three sides and three angles. The types of triangles are named according to the length of their sides and the size of their angles.

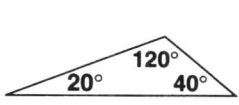 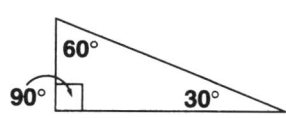 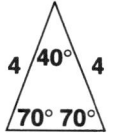 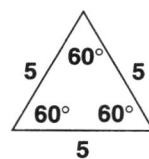

Scalene triangle
no equal sides
no equal angles

Right triangle
one 90°
(right) angle

Isosceles triangle
two equal sides
two equal angles

Equilateral triangle
three equal sides
three equal angles

Write the name of each triangle. Some triangles have two names.

1.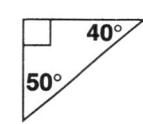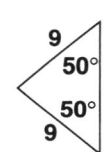

   right, isosceles   _____   _____

2.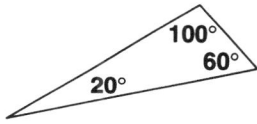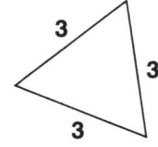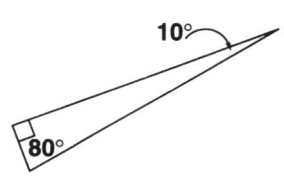

   _____   _____   _____

3.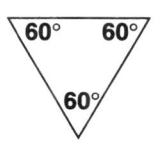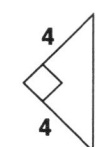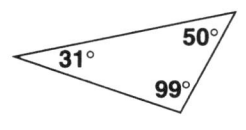

   _____   _____   _____

4.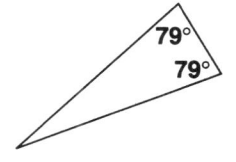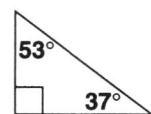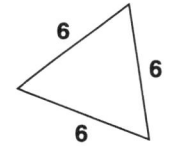

   _____   _____   _____

5. 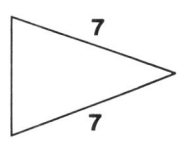   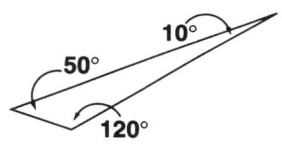

   _____   _____   _____

Triangles

The sum of the three angles in a triangle is 180°. To find the measure of any unknown angle in a triangle, add the measures of the two given angles and subtract the sum from 180°.

Find ∠A.

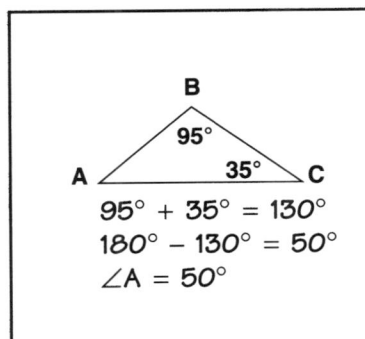

95° + 35° = 130°
180° − 130° = 50°
∠A = 50°

Find ∠R.

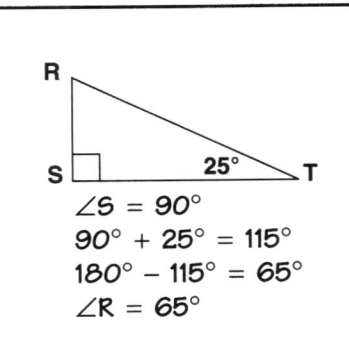

∠S = 90°
90° + 25° = 115°
180° − 115° = 65°
∠R = 65°

Find ∠M.

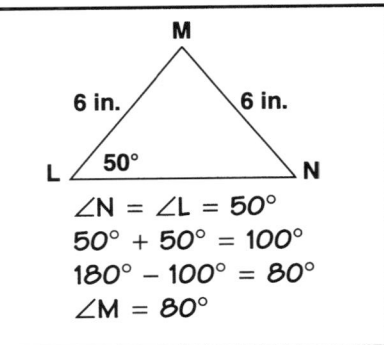

∠N = ∠L = 50°
50° + 50° = 100°
180° − 100° = 80°
∠M = 80°

Find the measure of each unknown angle.

1.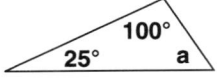

100° + 25° = 125°
180° − 125° = 55°
∠a = 55°

   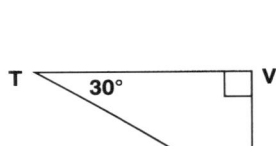

   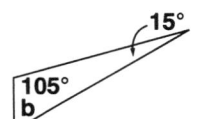

2.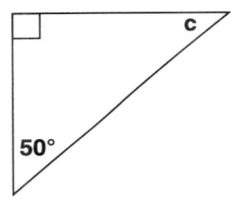

   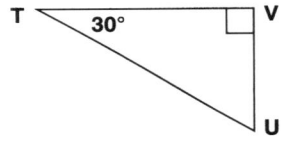

   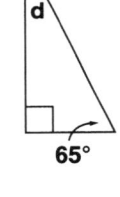

3.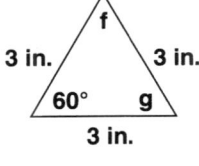

   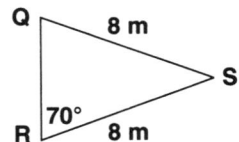

   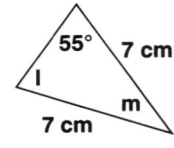

4.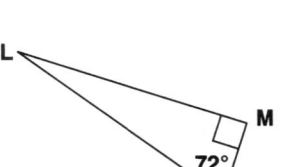

   (L, M, N triangle with 72° at N)

   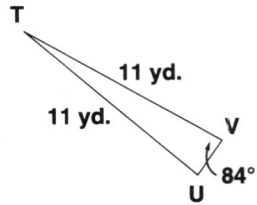

Similar Triangles

Similar triangles have the same shape and equal corresponding angles.

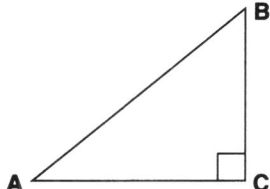 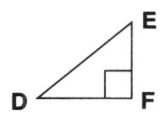

∠A = ∠D
∠B = ∠E
∠C = ∠F
△ABC ~ △DEF

The corresponding sides of similar triangles form equal ratios, or a proportion.

$$\frac{\overline{AB}}{\overline{DE}} = \frac{\overline{BC}}{\overline{EF}} = \frac{\overline{AC}}{\overline{DF}}$$

Find the length of $\overline{BC}$ in triangle ABC above if $\overline{AB}$ = 10, $\overline{DE}$ = 5, and $\overline{EF}$ = 3.

Write a proportion.	Substitute. Use n for the length of $\overline{BC}$.	Cross multiply to solve for $\overline{BC}$.
$\frac{\overline{AB}}{\overline{DE}} = \frac{\overline{BC}}{\overline{EF}}$	$\frac{10}{5} = \frac{n}{3}$	5n = 30 n = 30 ÷ 5 = 6 $\overline{BC}$ = 6

Find the length of n in each set of similar triangles.

1.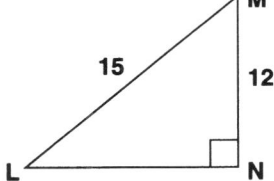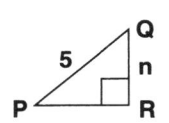

$\frac{\overline{LM}}{\overline{PQ}} = \frac{\overline{MN}}{\overline{QR}}$ $\frac{15}{5} = \frac{12}{n}$
15n = 60
n = 60 ÷ 15 = 4
$\overline{QR}$ = 4

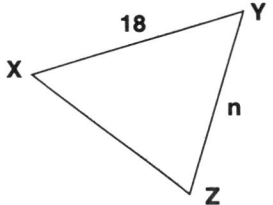 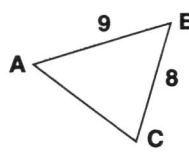

2.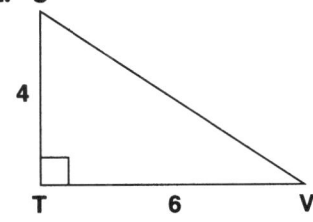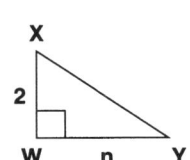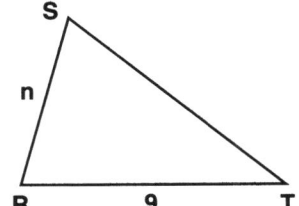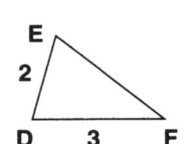

31

Pythagorean Theorem

The Pythagorean Theorem shows how the lengths of the sides of a right triangle are related. If you know the lengths of the two shorter sides, called legs, you can find the length of the third side, called the hypotenuse. The hypotenuse is always opposite the right angle. Use the same formula if you have the length of the hypotenuse and the length of one of the legs to find the length of the other leg.

$a^2 + b^2 = c^2$

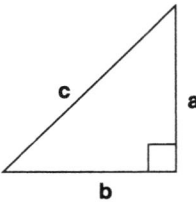

Find c if a = 3, b = 4.

$$a^2 + b^2 = c^2$$
$$3^2 + 4^2 = c^2$$
$$9 + 16 = c^2$$
$$25 = c^2$$
$$\sqrt{25} = c$$
$$5 = c$$

Find a if b = 6, c = 10.

$$a^2 + b^2 = c^2$$
$$a^2 + 6^2 = 10^2$$
$$a^2 + 36 = 100$$
$$a^2 = 100 - 36$$
$$a^2 = 64$$
$$a = \sqrt{64} = 8$$

Find the unknown side in each right triangle.

1.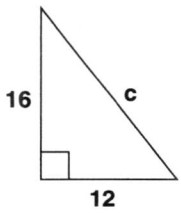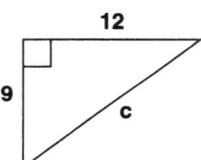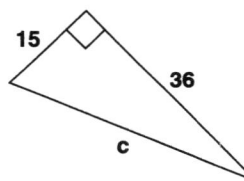

$$a^2 + b^2 = c^2$$
$$16^2 + 12^2 = c^2$$
$$256 + 144 = c^2$$
$$400 = c^2$$
$$\sqrt{400} = c$$
$$20 = c$$

2.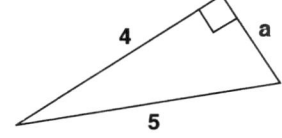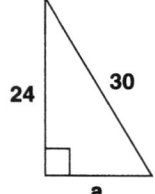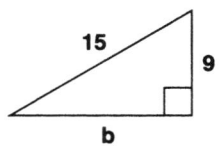

Checking Up

Find the measure of each unknown angle.

1.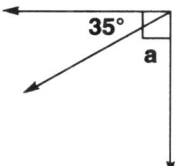

2.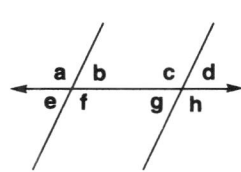

∠a = 100°	∠a =
∠b =	∠b = 72°
∠c =	∠c =
∠d =	∠d =
∠e =	∠e =
∠f =	∠f =
∠g =	∠g =
∠h =	∠h =

3.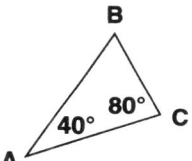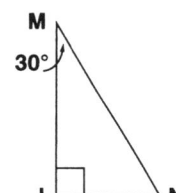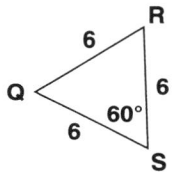

Find the length of n in each figure below.

4.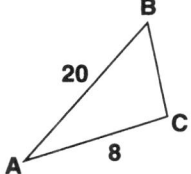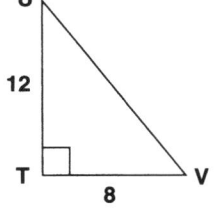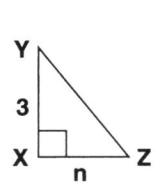

Solve.

5. Find the hypotenuse of a right triangle with legs that are 24 inches and 10 inches long.

   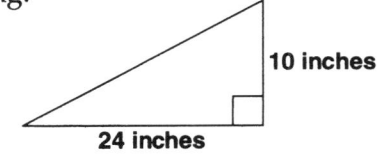

   Answer _____

6. Find the length of the straight line distance from point A to point B across a field that measures 9 yards by 12 yards.

   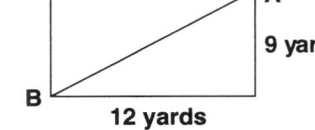

   Answer _____

Polygons

Flat figures with many sides and angles are called polygons.

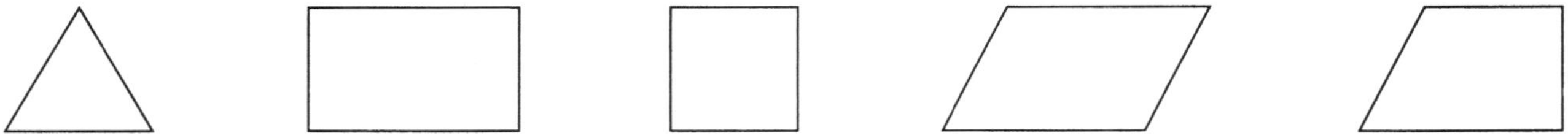

Triangle
3 sides
3 angles

Rectangle
4 sides
4 angles

Square
4 equal sides

Parallelogram
2 pairs of parallel sides

Trapezoid
1 pair of parallel sides

Write the name of each polygon.

1. 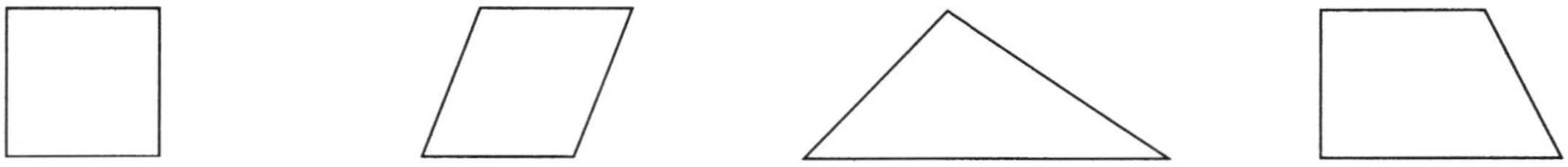 square / parallelogram / triangle / trapezoid

2. 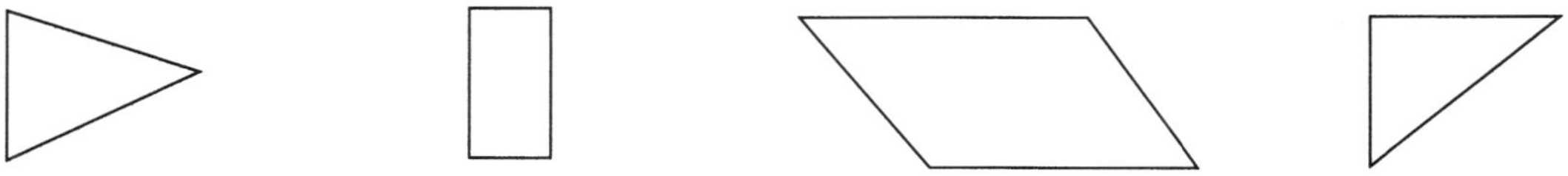 triangle / rectangle / parallelogram / triangle

3. trapezoid / square / rectangle / square

4.  rectangle / triangle / square / trapezoid

5. rectangle / trapezoid / triangle / square

Regular Polygons

Regular polygons have equal sides and equal angles.

Equilateral triangle
3 equal sides
3 equal angles

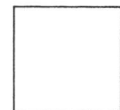
Square
4 equal sides
4 equal angles

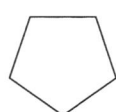
Pentagon
5 equal sides
5 equal angles

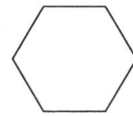
Hexagon
6 equal sides
6 equal angles

Heptagon
7 equal sides
7 equal angles

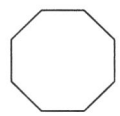
Octagon
8 equal sides
8 equal angles

Write the name of each polygon.

1.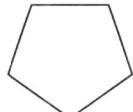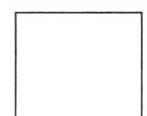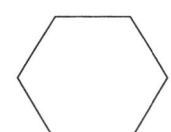

   pentagon _____   _____   _____   _____

2.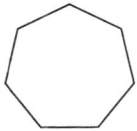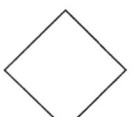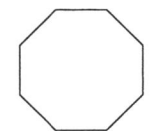

   _____   _____   _____   _____

3.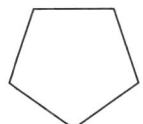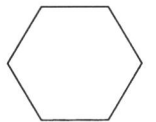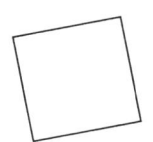

   _____   _____   _____   _____

4.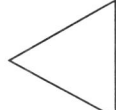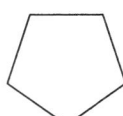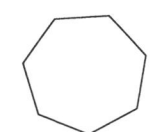

   _____   _____   _____   _____

Perimeter

To find the perimeter, or the measure of the distance around the outside of a figure, add the lengths of the sides. There are also formulas that show a shorter way to find the perimeter of a square or a rectangle.

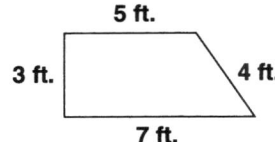

Polygon
$P = S_1 + S_2 + S_3 + S_4$
$P = 3 + 4 + 5 + 7 = 19$ ft.

Rectangle
$P = 2l + 2w$
$P = (2 \times 6) + (2 \times 4) = 20$ in.

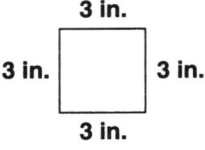

Square
$P = 4s$
$P = 4 \times 3 = 12$ in.

Find the perimeter of each figure.

1.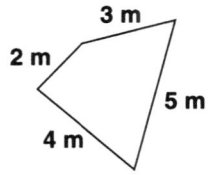

   $P = 2 + 3 + 4 + 5 = 14$ m

   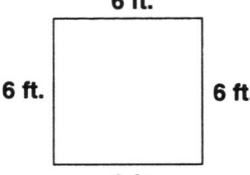

2.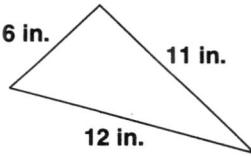

   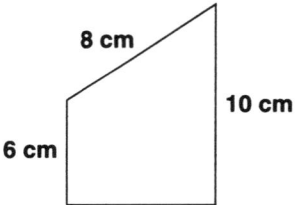

   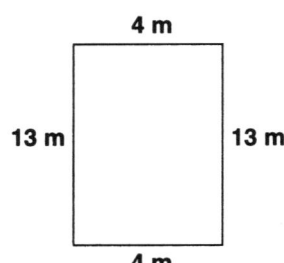

3.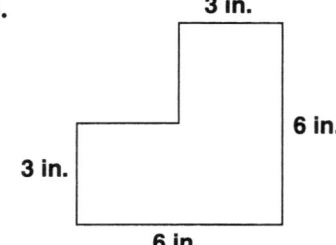

   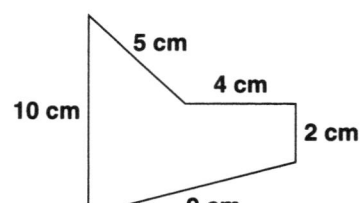

   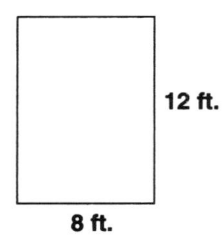

Solve.

4. If a rectangular room measures 12 feet wide by 15 feet long, what is the perimeter of the room?

   Answer _____

5. A square storage shed measures 20 meters on each side. What is the perimeter of the storage shed?

   Answer _____

Area

Formulas are also used to find the area, or the measure of the space inside a flat figure. Area is measured in square units.

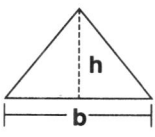
Triangle
$A = \frac{1}{2} bh$

Square
$A = s^2$

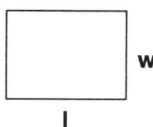
Rectangle
$A = lw$

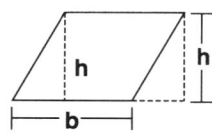
Parallelogram
$A = bh$

Find the area of the rectangle.

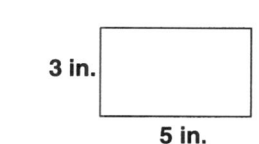

Write the formula.   Substitute.   Multiply.

$A = lw$ $A = 3 \times 5$ $A = 15$ sq. in.

Find the area of each figure.

1.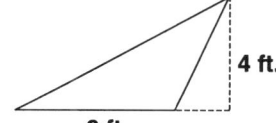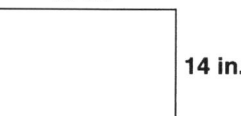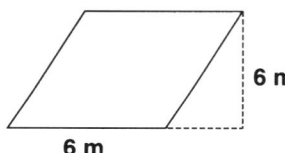

$A = \frac{1}{2} bh$
$A = \frac{1}{2} \times 6 \times 4 = 12$ sq. ft.

2.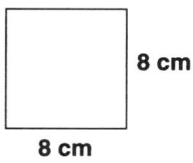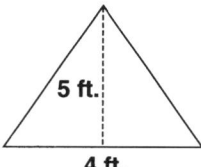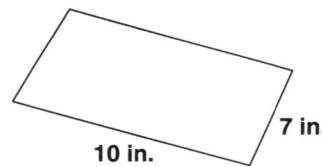

3.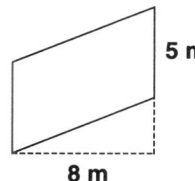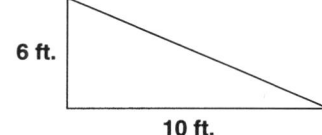

Solve.

4. A rectangular garage measures 9 feet wide by 12 feet long. What is the area of the garage?

   Answer _____

5. A farmer's field measures 100 yards by 100 yards. What is the area of the field?

   Answer _____

37

Area

Sometimes you will need to combine the areas of two or more figures in finding the total area of a construction or landscaping project.

Greg is adding a small storage room on to the side of his office. What is the total area of the office and the storage room?

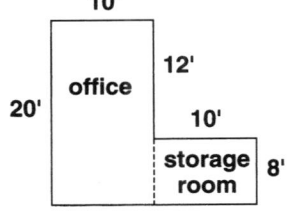

There are two ways to solve this problem. Find the area of the 20' by 20' square and subtract the area of the 12' by 10' rectangle not included in the total area.

The second way is to divide the figure into two rectangles. One rectangle is 8' by 10' and the other is 10' by 20'. Find the area of each rectangle and add to find the total area.

```
Area of square          Area of rectangle
A = s²                  A = lw
A = 20 × 20             A = 12 × 10
A = 400 sq. ft.         A = 120 sq. ft.

Subtract the areas.
400 − 120 = 280 sq. ft.
```

```
Area of first           Area of second
rectangle               rectangle
A = lw                  A = lw
A = 8 × 10              A = 10 × 20
A = 80 sq. ft.          A = 200 sq. ft.

Add the areas.
80 + 200 = 280 sq. ft.
```

Find the area of each figure.

1.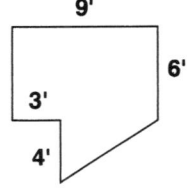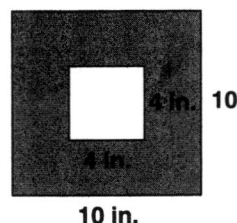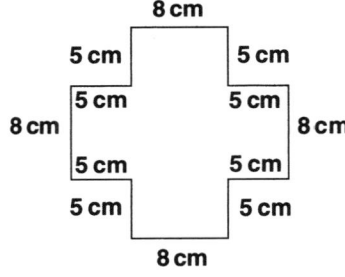

Solve.

2. The square carpet in a room 15 feet long on each side covers all but a 2-foot border on each side of the room. What is the total area of the carpet?

   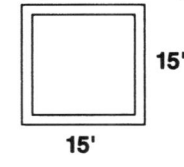

   Answer _____

3. A triangular flower bed is divided into four equal sections. A different kind of flower will be planted in each section. What is the area of each section?

   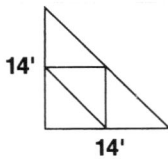

   Answer _____

Circumference and Area of Circles

The formulas for finding the circumference, or the distance around a circle, and the area of a circle use the math constant π (pi). Use 3.14 or $\frac{22}{7}$ for π.

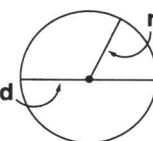

r = radius
d = diameter
d = 2r

Circumference
C = πd
C = 2πr

Area
A = πr²

Find the circumference. Use π = 3.14.

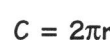

C = 2πr
C = 2 × 3.14 × 3
C = 18.84 in.

Find the area. Use π = $\frac{22}{7}$.

A = πr²
A = $\frac{22}{7}$ × 7 × 7
A = 154 square meters

Find the circumference and area of each circle. Use π = 3.14.

1.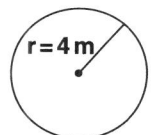

C = 2πr   A = πr²
C = 2 × 3.14 × 4   A = 3.14 × 4 × 4
C = 25.12 m   A = 50.24 square meters

Find the circumference and area of each circle. Use π = $\frac{22}{7}$.

2.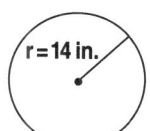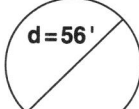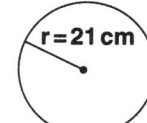

Solve.

3. A circular platform has a diameter of 20'. What is the area of the platform?

   Answer _____

4. A circular fountain has a diameter of 12 feet. A 2-foot wide path surrounds the fountain. What is the total area of the fountain and the path around it?

   Answer _____

39

Volume

Volume is the measure of the space inside a three-dimensional or solid figure. Volume is measured in cubic units.

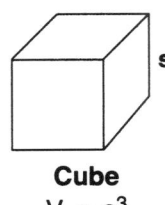
Cube
$V = s^3$

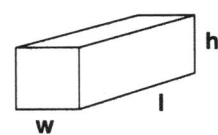
Rectangular Solid
$V = lwh$

Cylinder
$V = \pi r^2 h$

Find the volume of the cube.

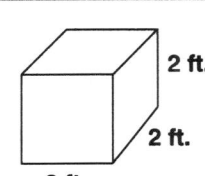

Write the formula.

$V = s^3$

Substitute. Multiply.

$V = 2^3$
$V = 2 \times 2 \times 2$
$V = 8$ cubic feet

Find the volume of each figure. Use $\pi = 3.14$.

1.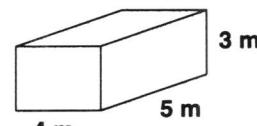
$V = lwh$
$V = 5 \times 4 \times 3 = 60$ cubic meters

   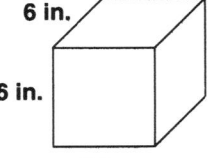

   $r = 3$ ft., $h = 4$ ft.

2.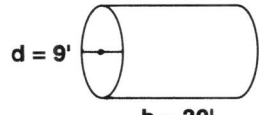
$d = 9'$, $h = 30'$

   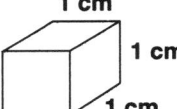
   1 cm × 1 cm × 1 cm

   5 m, 4 m, 6 m

3.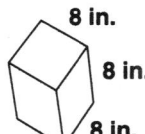
8 in. × 8 in. × 8 in.

   $r = 1$ in., 10 in.

   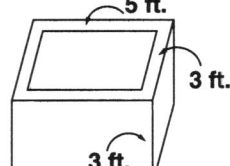
   5 ft., 3 ft., 3 ft.

Solve.

4. A concrete brick measures 8 inches by 3 inches by 2 inches. What is the volume of the brick?

   Answer _____

5. A cylindrical mailing tube has a diameter of 4 inches and a length of 36 inches. What is the volume of the tube?

   Answer _____

Checking Up

Find the perimeter and area of each figure.

1.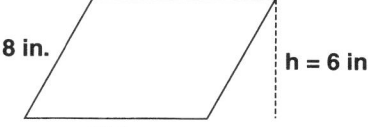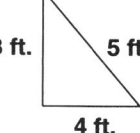

Find the circumference and area of each circle. Find the volume of the cylinder. Use π = 3.14.

2.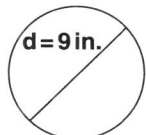

Find the volume of each solid.

3.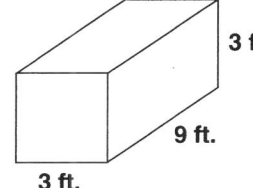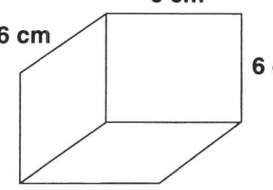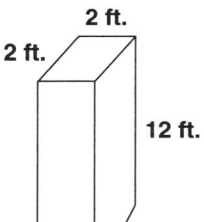

Solve.

4. A rectangular boxcar is 40 feet by 10 feet by 8 feet. What is the volume of the boxcar?

   Answer _____

5. A cylindrical water tank has an inside diameter of 12 feet. The tank is 5 feet high. What is the volume of the tank?

   Answer _____

41

Coordinate Geometry

The rectangular coordinate system has a horizontal *x*-axis and a vertical *y*-axis that cross at the origin and that divide the plane into four quadrants, labeled I, II, III, and IV.

Each point in the plane can be assigned coordinates (*x*,*y*) that show where the point is located. On the *x*-axis, positive numbers are counted to the right and negative numbers are counted to the left. On the *y*-axis, positive numbers are counted up and negative numbers are counted down. The *x*-coordinate is always written first.

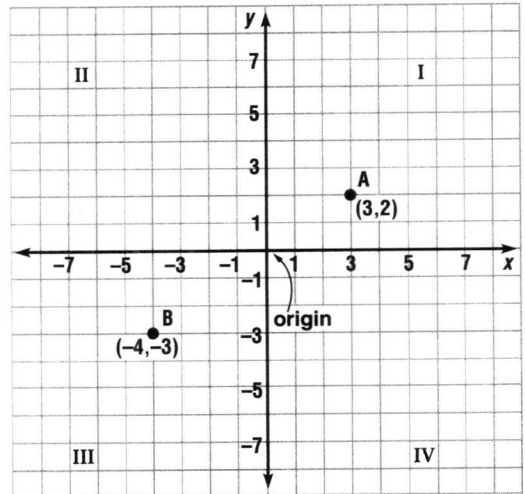

Point A has coordinates (3,2) and is located in Quadrant I.

Point B has coordinates (–4,–3) and is located in Quadrant III.

Find the coordinates of each of the points shown on the coordinate system. Identify the quadrant in which each point is located.

1. Point A
   (4,1)
   Quadrant I

   Point B

2. Point C   Point D

3. Point E   Point F

4. Point G   Point H

5. Point I   Point J

6. Point K   Point L

42

Coordinate Geometry

To plot a point with coordinates (x,y), first move right or left to find the value of the x-coordinate on the x-axis. Then move up or down to find the value of the y-coordinate.

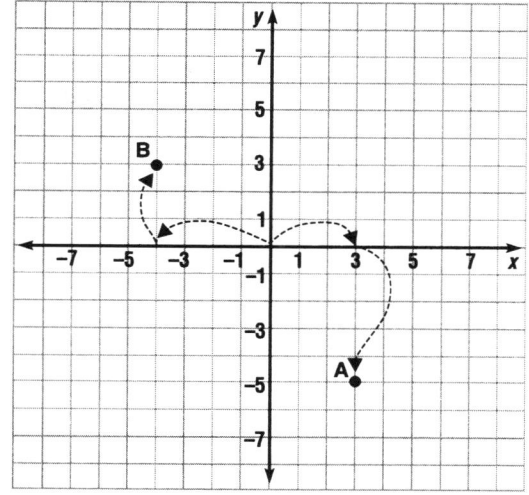

To plot the point (3,−5) find 3 on the x-axis. Move down 5 because y is negative. The point is labeled A. To plot the point (−4,3), find −4 on the x-axis. Move up 3 because y is positive. This point is labeled B.

Plot each point on the coordinate axis. Label each point.

1. A (3,4)   B (−5,3)

2. C (−4,−1)   D (6,−4)

3. E (−1,5)   F (−7,−3)

4. G (4,5)   H (−6,3)

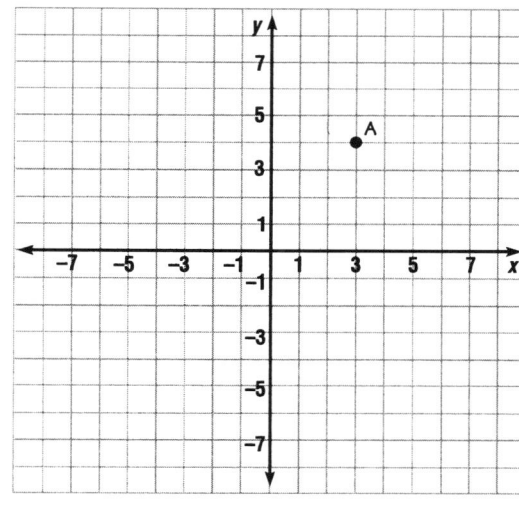

Plot and label each point.

5. A (5,5)   B (5,−5)
   C (−5,−5)   D (−5,5)

6. Connect points A, B, C, D, and A in order. Name the figure.

7. What is the length of each side of the figure?

8. Find the perimeter and the area of the figure.

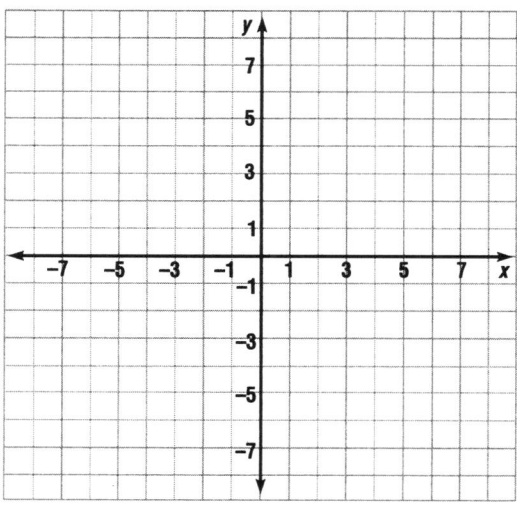

43

Progress Review

Change each measurement to the unit given.

1. 50 oz. = _____ lb. $4\frac{1}{2}$ hr. = _____ hr. _____ min.   6 gal. = _____ qt.

2. 12 c. = _____ pt.   5 yr. 6 mo. = _____ yr.   5 yd. = _____ in.

3. 3,000 m = _____ km   1.4 g = _____ mg   39 cL = _____ L

Add, subtract, multiply, or divide. Simplify if possible.

4.   3 lb. 14 oz.   30 min. 10 sec.   500 m + 2 km = _____ km
   + 5 lb. 12 oz.   − 10 min. 30 sec.

5. 96 L ÷ 30 = _____ cL   6 c. 4 fl. oz.   5)‾21 yd. 2 ft.
                           ×   4

Find the measure of each unknown angle.

6.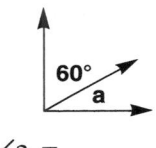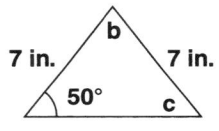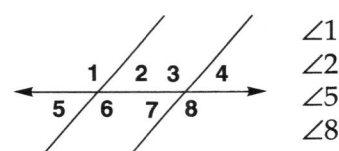

∠a =   ∠b =   ∠1 = 105°
                    ∠c =   ∠2 =
                                        ∠5 =
                                        ∠8 =

Find the length of x in each figure below.

7.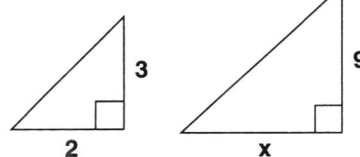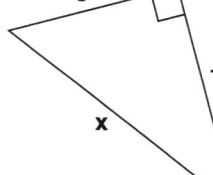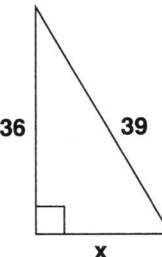

Solve.

8. John's son is 67 inches tall. His daughter is 4 feet 10 inches tall. Which one of John's children is taller?

   Answer _____

9. A delivery service will deliver packages that weigh 25 pounds or less. Will they deliver a package of computer disks that weighs 500 ounces?

   Answer _____

Find the perimeter, or circumference, and the area of each figure. Use π = 3.14.

10.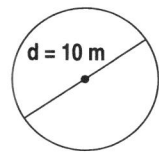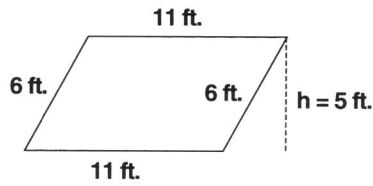

Find the volume of each figure. Use π = 3.14.

11.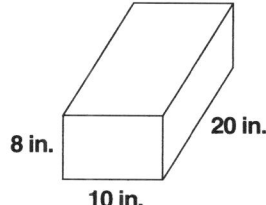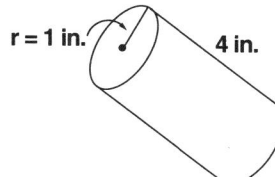

Find the coordinates of each point.

12. A   B   C

Plot the points on the coordinate system.

13. D (–5,–2)   E (4,3)   F (1,–1)

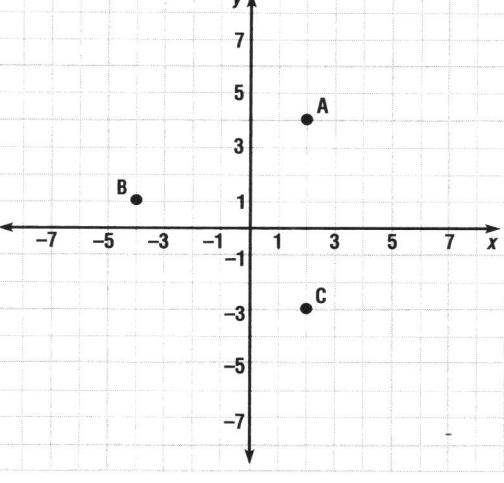

Find the area of each figure. Use π = $\frac{22}{7}$.

14.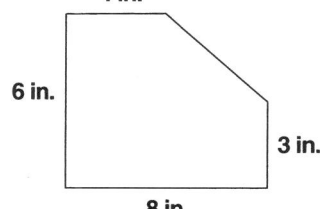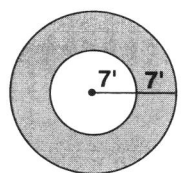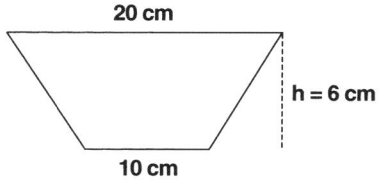

Solve.

15. The Westside Recreation Center built a new swimming pool that measures 20 feet by 15 feet. Find the perimeter and the area of the pool.

    Answer _____

16. Find the volume of the pool if the pool is 6 feet deep.

    Answer _____

45

ANSWER KEY

Page 2
1. 12 in. 12 in. 3 ft.
2. 1 yd. 1 yd. 1 ft.
3. 5,280 ft. 5,280 ft. 1,760 yd.
4. 1 mi. 1 mi. 1 mi.
5. $\frac{1}{12}$ ft. $\frac{1}{3}$ yd. $\frac{1}{12}$ ft.
6. $\frac{1}{5,280}$ mi. $\frac{1}{1,760}$ mi. $\frac{1}{5,280}$ mi.
7. $\frac{1}{3}$ yd. $\frac{1}{1,760}$ mi. $\frac{1}{36}$ yd.
8. $\frac{1}{3}$ yard 9. 1 mile

Page 3
1. 18 ft. 100 in. 15,840 ft.
2. 51 in. 1 ft. 8,800 yd.
3. 880 yd. 72 in. 5 ft.
4. $3\frac{1}{3}$ ft. $5\frac{1}{3}$ yd. $1\frac{1}{2}$ mi.
5. $1\frac{1}{3}$ yd. $1\frac{1}{6}$ ft. $1\frac{7}{18}$ yd.
6. 2 mi. $\frac{1}{3}$ yd. 12 yd.
7. 72 inches 8. 10 yards

Page 4
1. 1 lb. 1 lb. 2,000 lb.
2. 16 oz. 16 oz. 1 T.
3. $\frac{1}{16}$ lb. $\frac{1}{2,000}$ T. $\frac{1}{2,000}$ T.
4. $\frac{1}{16}$ lb. 1 lb. 1 oz.
5. 1 pound 6. 2,000 pounds
7. 16 ounces 8. 1 ton

Page 5
1. 12,000 lb. 132 oz. 8 oz.
2. 68 oz. 10,000 lb. 500 lb.
3. 32 oz. 12 oz. 6,500 lb.
4. $2\frac{1}{2}$ lb. $\frac{3}{16}$ lb. $2\frac{1}{2}$ T.
5. 2 lb. $\frac{1}{2}$ T. $\frac{1}{20}$ T.
6. $\frac{3}{4}$ T. $\frac{1}{8}$ lb. $8\frac{3}{4}$ T.
7. $1\frac{1}{8}$ pounds 8. 25,000 pounds

Page 6
1. 8 fl. oz. 8 fl. oz. 1 pt.
2. 4 c. 1 qt. 1 qt.
3. 1 c. 1 qt. 4 qt.
4. 1 qt. 2 pt. 1 gal.
5. $\frac{1}{8}$ c. $\frac{1}{4}$ gal. $\frac{1}{4}$ qt.
6. $\frac{1}{4}$ qt. $\frac{1}{2}$ qt. $\frac{1}{8}$ c.
7. $\frac{1}{2}$ qt. $\frac{1}{4}$ gal. $\frac{1}{2}$ pt.
8. 1 cup 9. 1 quart

Page 7
1. 17 c. 10 qt. 40 fl. oz.
2. 18 c. 1 c. 28 fl. oz.
3. 20 qt. 3 qt. 4 c.
4. $1\frac{1}{2}$ qt. 10 gal. 8 pt.
5. $1\frac{1}{2}$ qt. 3 qt. $\frac{1}{2}$ c.
6. $2\frac{1}{2}$ pt. $1\frac{3}{4}$ qt. $1\frac{1}{2}$ c.
7. $2\frac{1}{2}$ cups 8. 24 pints

Page 8
1. 60 sec. 60 sec. 24 hr.
2. 52 wk. 52 wk. 12 mo.
3. 1 wk. 1 yr. 1 yr.
4. 1 min. 1 hr. 1 day
5. $\frac{1}{24}$ day $\frac{1}{7}$ wk. $\frac{1}{12}$ yr.
6. $\frac{1}{52}$ yr. $\frac{1}{12}$ yr. $\frac{1}{7}$ wk.
7. 1 hour 8. $\frac{1}{12}$ year

Page 9
1. 480 min. 204 hr. 30 mo.
2. 255 sec. 156 wk. 96 hr.
3. 105 days 360 min. 300 sec.
4. $1\frac{1}{3}$ hr. $1\frac{1}{3}$ yr. $1\frac{1}{2}$ min.
5. 4 yr. $1\frac{1}{4}$ hr. $\frac{1}{3}$ day
6. 2 yr. $\frac{1}{4}$ yr. 2 days
7. $1\frac{5}{6}$ years 8. 240 seconds

Page 10
1. 8 in. < 1 ft.
   3 c. < 1 qt.
   22 oz. > 1 lb.
2. 72 hr. = 3 days
   5 yd. < 20 ft.
   2 T. > 1,750 lb.
3. 150 min. > 2 hr.
   $2\frac{1}{2}$ gal. > 5 qt.
   5 mi. > 15,840 ft.
4. 8 wk. < 60 days
   $3\frac{1}{4}$ lb. > 50 oz.
   $6\frac{1}{2}$ pt. > 3 qt.
5. 70 in. > $1\frac{1}{3}$ yd.
   16 fl. oz. = 2 c.
   150 sec. < 3 min.
6. 3 lb. = 48 oz.
   $\frac{1}{2}$ mi. < 3,000 ft.
   6 qt. < 2 gal.
7. $2\frac{1}{2}$ hr. = 150 min.
   32 oz. > $1\frac{1}{2}$ lb.
   $\frac{1}{2}$ gal. < 3 qt.
8. no 9. Wednesday

Page 11
1. 1 yd. 1 ft. 2 lb. 4 oz.
2. 4 gal. 2 qt. 3 hr. 30 min.
3. 10 ft. 4 in. 2 qt. 1 pt.
4. 5 yr. 9 mo. 1 T. 200 lb.
5. 4 pt. 1 c. 2 mi. 1,056 ft.
6. 2 lb. 4 oz. 6 days 8 hr.
7. 5 minutes 45 seconds
8. 2 feet 6 inches

Page 12
1. 1 yd. 3 in. 4 days 4 hr.
2. 7 pt. 1 c. 2 lb. 8 oz.
3. 1 mi. 352 yd. 2 gal. 3 qt.
4. 3 hr. 15 min. 1 T. 1,050 lb.
5. 8 qt. 1 pt. 4 yr. 2 mo.
6. 1 lb. 6 oz. 6 yd. 1 ft.
7. 1 yr. 26 wk. 3 mi. 528 ft.
8. 2 T. 1,200 lb. 3 c. 6 fl. oz.
9. 3 min. 20 sec. 5 yd. 1 ft.
10. 5 feet 10 inches
11. 1 year 6 months

Page 13
1. 7 pt. $5\frac{1}{8}$ lb. 160 min.
2. $6\frac{1}{4}$ ft. 3 c. $1\frac{1}{4}$ T.
3. 38 days $6\frac{1}{2}$ mi. 11 qt.
4. $1\frac{3}{4}$ lb. 87 hr. $7\frac{1}{3}$ yd.
5. 30 fl. oz. 4,200 lb. $3\frac{1}{6}$ min.
6. 98 in. $5\frac{1}{2}$ qt. 52 oz.
7. 200 ounces 8. $6\frac{2}{3}$ yards

Page 14
1. 1 ft. 3 ft. $\frac{1}{2}$ mi.
2. 66 in. 5,720 yd. 1 lb.
3. 4 oz. 48 oz. 6 qt.
4. 4 c. 2 qt. $\frac{1}{2}$ pt.
5. $1\frac{1}{4}$ c. 3 qt. 1 hr.
6. 26 wk. 63 days 75 min.
7. 20 in. > $1\frac{1}{2}$ ft.
   2 hr. = 120 min.
   50 oz. < $3\frac{1}{2}$ lb.
8. 3 c. 4 fl. oz. 7 lb. 4 oz.
9. 2 yd. 18 in. 1 hr. 15 min.
10. 6 ft. 8 in. 1 yr. 2 mo.
11. 4 T. 1,000 lb. 3 gal. 3 qt.
12. 11 c. 83 oz.
13. 132 hr. 28 in.
14. 5 pounds 8 ounces
15. Sun City

Page 15
1. 7 c. 2 fl. oz.
   6 yd.
   9 days
2. 3 T. 1,500 lb.
   3 qt. 1 pt.
   9 mi. 1,000 yd.
3. 20 hr. 30 min.
   13 lb. 8 oz.
   22 gal. 3 qt.
4. 3 ft. 36 min. 5 sec.
5. 7 T. 5 gal. 1 qt.
6. 4 yd. 18 lb. 2 oz.
7. 6 pounds 8. 14 hours 20 minutes

Page 16
1. 10 in. 0 pt. 9 oz.
2. 1 min. 45 sec.
   3 yd.
   4 pt.
3. 10 yr. 6 mo.
   4 ft. 9 in.
   4 gal. 3 qt.
4. 1 T. 1,500 lb. 4 days 20 hr.
5. 1 mi. 4,280 ft. 6 yd. 2 ft.
6. 8 inches 7. 2 quarts

Page 17
1. 13 lb.
   1 hr. 3 min.
   13 ft. 6 in.
2. 4 c. 1 fl. oz.
   3 days 14 hr.
   13 ft. 4 in.
3. 10 gal. 2 qt.
   1 day 16 hr.
   15 yr.
4. 8 gal. 3 qt. 14 T. 16 mi.
5. 12 lb. 30 days 72 yd.
6. 5 gal. 2 qt. 3 yd. 9 T.
7. 6 feet 8. 4 hours 30 minutes

Page 18
1. 1 c. 7 fl. oz.
   1 lb. 5 oz.
   1 hr. 15 min.
2. 1 yd. 26 in.
   1 qt. 1 pt.
   2 T. 250 lb.

3. 2 days 15 hr.
   2 mi. 440 ft.
   2 gal. 1 qt.
4. 1 ton 500 pounds
5. 2 feet 7 inches

Page 19
1. 12 lb.　　9 yd.　　1 gal.
2. 13 yr. 2 mo.　　7 gal.
3. 7 in.
   2 gal. 2 qt.
   2 wk. 5 days
4. 4 T. 1,500 lb.　　2 yd. 35 in.
5. 13 qt.
   41 days
   6 mi. 1,320 ft.
6. 38 yd.　　9 gal. 3 qt.　　5 mi.
7. 1 hr. 15 min.
   1 T. 250 lb.
   2 pt. 1 c.
8. 2 mi. 528 yd.
   2 lb. 2 oz.
   20 min.
9. 4 hours 30 minutes
10. 13 ounces

Page 20
1. 34,000 dL　139 g　　15,700 mm
2. 2,700 mL　1,000 dg　3,000 cm
3. 3.45 dL　　50,000 mm　　2 g
4. 150 m < 15 km
   3.2 cL < 320 dL
   5 mg = 0.5 cg
5. 1 km > 100 m
   4.5 L > 45 mL
   7 g > 700 mg
6. 1,000 milliliters
7. 3.5-kilometer trail

Page 21
1. 10 kL　　30 m　　111.5 cg
2. .3 daL　　1.5 km　　.04 g
3. 520 L　　36 cm　　6 kg
4. 4,500 mL < 45 L
   1.5 km > 150 cm
   10,000 mg = 1 dag
5. 5 L > 50 mL
   18 dm = 1.8 m
   0.7 kg > 7 g
6. 5 kilograms　　7. 1.5-liter bottle

Page 22
1. 43 cm　　496 cg　　990 L
2. 22 dm　　.68 kg　　25 L
3. 8 m　　.5 kg　　15.6 kL
4. 9 hm　　65 cL　　81 dg
5. 1.1 m　　900 g　　47.5 cL
6. 11.6 g　　693 L　　10.1 hm
7. 2 km　　9.2 g　　4 L
8. 4.2 grams　　9. 9.7 meters

Page 23
1. 1.75 kg　　4 cL　　4.34 m
2. 400 mg　　10 L　　1 km
3. 2.16 dag　2 daL　　2 cm
4. .048 g　　300 mL　21.6 cm
5. 88 kg　　3.15 L　　20 m
6. 18.5 cg　13.15 daL　1.8 km
7. 1.2 g　　.5 cL　　63 mm
8. .018 kiloliters
9. 2,500 milligrams

Page 24
1. 5,900 m
   9,000 mL
   60,000 mg
2. 1,000 mm　　730 L　　4,000 cg
3. 310 cm　　20 dL　　800 g
4. 5 km　　　.3 L　　6 dg
5. 8.8 m　　　.1 kL　　9.3 dag
6. 20 dm　　.5 hL　　320,000 g
7. 20 m < 2 km
   500 cL < 5 kL
   160 cg = 1.6 g
8. 3,500 mm > 3.5 dm
   6 L < 0.6 hL
   900,000 mg = 0.9 kg
9. 4.5 m　　18 L　　2 kg
10. 2 m　　　0 dL　　7.5 dag
11. 15 dm　　14 kL　　1.9 kg
12. .04 dam　　.2 L　　5,000 g
13. 3 kilometers　14. 524 grams

Page 25
1. acute angle　　right angle
   right angle　　intersecting lines
2. perpendicular lines
   parallel lines
   straight angle　　obtuse angle
3. right angle　　acute angle
   intersecting lines　　parallel lines
4. ∠Y or ∠XYZ　　∠U or ∠TUV
   ∠M or ∠LMN　∠a
5. parallel　　6. right

Page 26
1. ∠a = 145°, obtuse; ∠b = 35°, acute
   ∠p = 50°, acute; ∠q = 130°, obtuse
2. ∠x = 90°, right; ∠y = 90°, right
   ∠R = 120°, obtuse; ∠S = 60°, acute
3. ∠l = 100°, obtuse; ∠m = 80°, acute
   ∠U = 45°, acute; ∠V = 135°, obtuse

Page 27
1. ∠ZXY = 25°
   ∠a = 60°
   ∠DBC = 45°
2. ∠MKL = 150°
   ∠b = 10°
   ∠SQR = 75°
3. ∠WUT = 75°
   ∠d = 150°
   ∠DBC = 35°
4. ∠XYW = 50°
   ∠y = 90°
   ∠KIJ = 170°

Page 28
1. ∠b = ∠d = 140°, ∠c = 40°
   ∠d = 100°, ∠a = ∠c = 80°
   ∠a = 50°, ∠b = ∠d = 130°
2. ∠b = 110°, ∠a = ∠c = 70°
   ∠c = 35°, ∠b = ∠d = 145°
   ∠d = 107°, ∠a = ∠c = 73°
3. ∠1 = ∠4 = ∠5 = ∠8 = 95°,
   ∠2 = ∠3 = ∠6 = ∠7 = 85°
   ∠2 = ∠3 = ∠6 = ∠7 = 75°,
   ∠1 = ∠4 = ∠5 = ∠8 = 105°
   ∠2 = ∠3 = ∠6 = ∠7 = 88°,
   ∠1 = ∠4 = ∠5 = ∠8 = 92°
4. ∠a = ∠c = ∠f = ∠h = 120°,
   ∠d = ∠e = ∠g = 60°

Page 29
1. right, isosceles
   right
   equilateral
2. scalene　　right　　isosceles
3. equilateral
   right, isosceles
   right
4. isosceles　right　　scalene
5. isosceles　scalene　equilateral

Page 30
1. ∠a = 55°　∠Y = 95°　∠b = 60°
2. ∠c = 40°　∠U = 60°　∠d = 25°
3. ∠f = ∠g = 60°
   ∠Q = 70°, ∠S = 40°
   ∠l = 55°, ∠m = 70°
4. ∠E = 111°
   ∠L = 18°
   ∠U = 84°, ∠T = 12°

Page 31
1. n = 4　　n = 16
2. n = 3　　n = 6

Page 32
1. c = 20　c = 13　c = 15　c = 39
2. a = 3　b = 12　a = 18　b = 12

Page 33
1. ∠a = 55°　∠OMN = 70°
   ∠f = 50°　∠TRS = 148°
2. ∠a = ∠c = ∠f = ∠h = 100°,
   ∠b = ∠d = ∠e = ∠g = 80°,
   ∠b = ∠d = ∠e = ∠g = 72°,
   ∠a = ∠c = ∠f = ∠h = 108°
3. ∠B = 60°
   ∠E = 80°, ∠F = 50°
   ∠N = 60°
   ∠Q = ∠R = 60°
4. n = 4　　n = 2
5. 26 inches　　6. 15 yards

Page 34
1. square　　　parallelogram
   triangle　　　trapezoid
2. triangle　　　rectangle
   parallelogram　triangle
3. trapezoid　　square
   rectangle　　parallelogram
4. rectangle　　triangle
   square　　　trapezoid
5. rectangle　　trapezoid
   triangle　　　square

Page 35
1. pentagon　　square
   triangle　　　hexagon
2. heptagon　　square
   octagon　　　triangle
3. pentagon　　octagon
   hexagon　　square
4. triangle　　　pentagon
   heptagon　　square

Page 36
1. 14 m　　24 ft.　　28 yd.
2. 29 in.　30 cm　　34 m
3. 24 in.　30 cm　　40 ft.
4. 54 feet　5. 80 meters

47

Page 37
1. 12 sq. ft.   266 sq. in.   36 sq. m
2. 64 sq. cm   10 sq. ft.   70 sq. in.
3. 40 sq. m   12 sq. cm   30 sq. ft.
4. 108 square feet
5. 10,000 square yards

Page 38
1. 66 sq. ft.   84 sq. in.   224 sq. cm
2. 121 square feet
3. 24.5 square feet

Page 39
1. C = 25.12 m; A = 50.24 sq. m
   C = 21.98 in.; A = 38.465 sq. in.
   C = 37.68 ft.; A = 113.04 sq. ft.
2. C = 88 in.; A = 616 sq. in.
   C = 176 ft.; A = 2,464 sq. ft.
   C = 132 cm; A = 1,386 sq. cm
3. 314 square feet
4. 200.96 square feet

Page 40
1. 60 cu. meters
   216 cu. in.
   113.04 cu. ft.
2. 1,907.55 cu. ft.
   1 cu. cm
   120 cu. m
3. 512 cu. in.
   31.4 cu. in.
   45 cu. ft.
4. 48 cubic inches
5. 452.16 cubic inches

Page 41
1. P = 40 in.; A = 72 sq. in.
   P = 12 ft.; A = 6 sq. ft.
   P = 28 m; A = 42 sq. m
2. C = 28.26 in.; A = 63.585 sq. in.
   C = 75.36 cm; A = 452.16 sq. cm
   V = 125.6 cu. ft.
3. 81 cu. ft.
   216 cu. cm
   48 cu. ft.
4. 3,200 cubic feet
5. 565.2 cubic feet

Page 42
1. (4,1); I   (−3,5); II
2. (−3,−3); III   (1,−7); IV
3. (2,4); I   (−4,2); II
4. (−6,−5); III   (3,−3); IV
5. (−7,−2); III   (5,6); I
6. (−6,6); II   (7,−4); IV

Page 43
1. – 4.

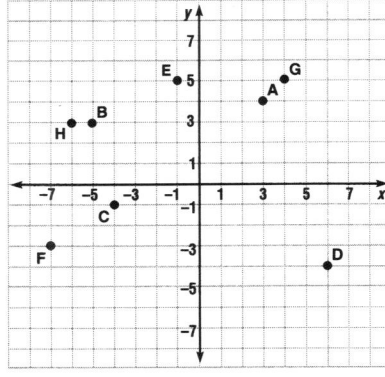

5. – 6.

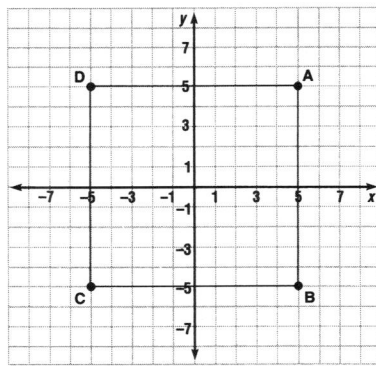

6. square   7. 10 units
8. P = 40 units;   A = 100 square units

Page 44
1. $3\frac{1}{8}$ lb.   4 hr. 30 min.   24 qt.
2. 6 pt. $5\frac{1}{2}$ yr.   180 in.
3. 3 km   1,400 mg   .39 L
4. 9 lb. 10 oz.
   19 min. 40 sec.
   2.5 km
5. 320 cL   26 c.   4 yd. 1 ft.
6. ∠a = 30°   ∠b = 80°, ∠c = 50°
   ∠1 = ∠8 = 105°, ∠2 = ∠5 = 75°
7. x = 6   x = 13   x = 15
8. John's son   9. no

Page 45
10. C = 31.4 m; A = 78.5 sq. m
    P = 32 in.; A = 64 sq. in.
    P = 34 ft.; A = 55 sq. ft.
11. 1,600 cu. in.
    64 cu. cm
    12.56 cu. in.
12. A (2,4)   B (−4,1)   C (2,−3)

13.

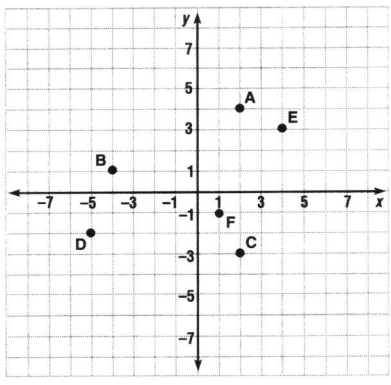

14. 42 sq. in.
    462 sq. ft.
    90 sq. cm
15. P = 70 feet; A = 300 square feet
16. V = 1,800 cubic feet